D0934157

THIS IS THE COCKER SPANIEL

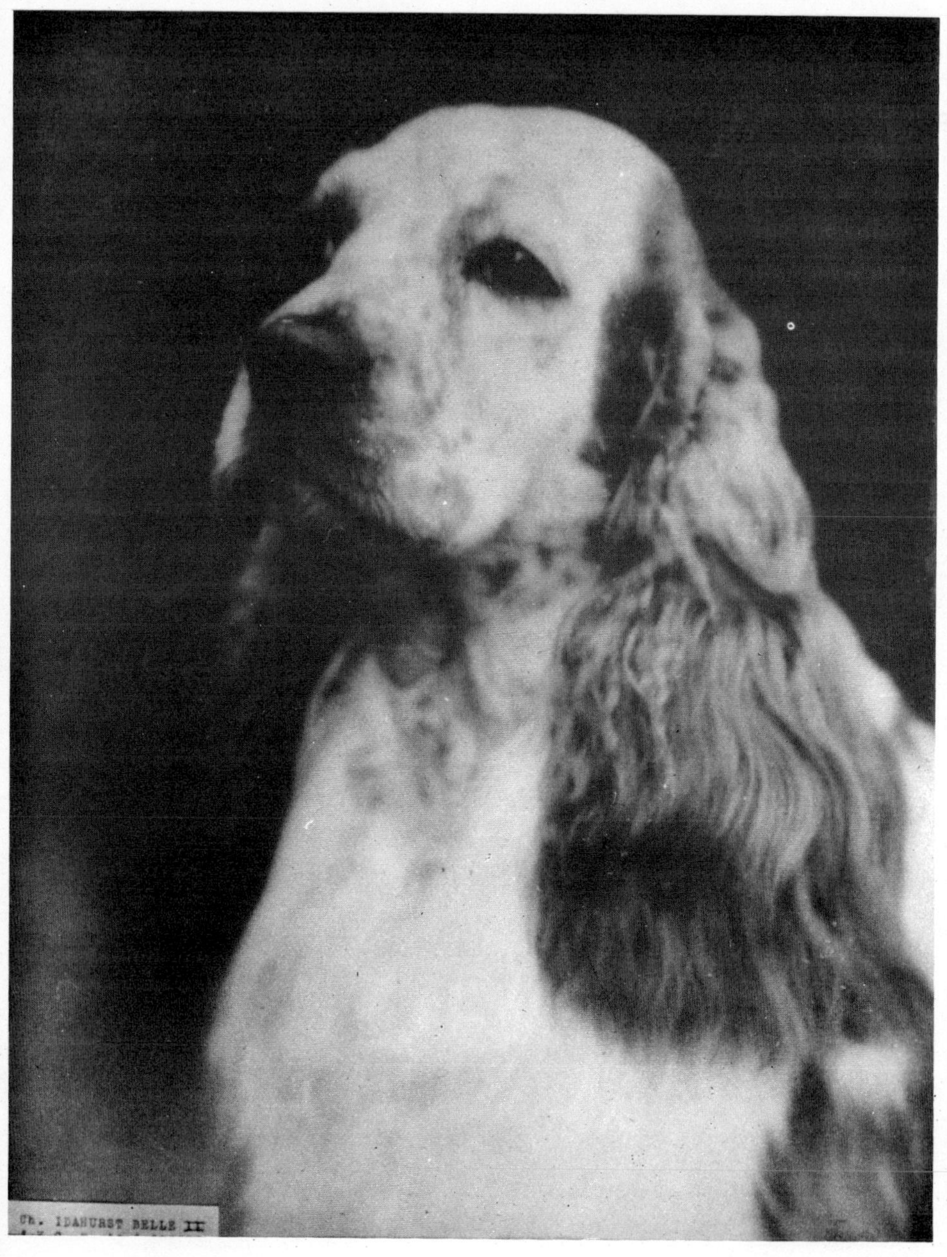

Idahurst Belle II. One of the Cockers which made thousands want to own one.

THIS IS THE
COCKER SPANIEL

by

Leon F. Whitney, D.V.M.

Illustrated by

Ernest H. Hart

Distributed in the U.S.A. by T.F.H. Publications, Inc., 211 West Sylvania Avenue, P.O. Box 27, Neptune City, N.J. 07753; in England by T.F.H. (Gt. Britain) Ltd., 13 Nutley Lane, Reigate, Surrey; in Canada to the book store and library trade by Clarke, Irwin & Company, Clarwin House, 791 St. Clair Avenue West, Toronto 10, Ontario; in Canada to the pet trade by Rolf C. Hagen Ltd., 3225 Sartelon Street, Montreal 382, Quebec; in Southeast Asia by Y.W. Ong, 9 Lorong 36 Geylang, Singapore 14; in Australia and the south Pacific by Pet Imports Pty. Ltd., P.O. Box 149, Brookvale 2100, N.S.W., Australia. Published by T.F.H. Publications, Inc. Ltd., The British Crown Colony of Hong Kong.

ISBN 0-87666-271-8

I am addressing this book to:

You who are expecting to buy a puppy;
You who have bought a Cocker Spaniel;
You who wish to start breeding a great type of dog and become identified with it (I hope you will do so); and
You who are already breeders and are able to see facts without rationalizing the unpleasant.

I am *not* addressing this book to:

The money breeders who have helped to deteriorate a once-great breed;
The Cocker breeders who are interested only in dog shows; or to
Those persons who use Cockers only to glorify themselves.

Note

What's happened to the Cocker?

I'm sure I know. And I'm going to tell you without fear of consequences. I admire Cockers. I believe, from having raised more than 2,000 and from having worked as a veterinarian, what thousands more believe—that the proper Cocker is the finest small dog ever developed for human companionship. I believe it will again go to the head of the registration list. You and I can put it there, if you, the breeder, will breed proper Cockers, and if you, Mr. and Mrs. Public, will buy only that kind.

CONTENTS

THIS IS THE COCKER SPANIEL

Chapter 1

THIS WAS THE COCKER

The Cocker Spaniel gained rapidly in popularity, to become the A number 1 dog, because it deserved to do so. When Idahurst Belle went Best in Madison Square Garden, the event rang the bell because the public realized that here was the ultimate in the perfect pet. Her prototype was sought everywhere.

I have known her and many of her descendants well, and everyone will agree with this: if we had such Cockers today there would be no decrease in registrations. And since I think Belle came as near as possible to both the perfect house dog and hunting companion, I shall describe her as epitomizing the perfect Cocker.

Belle was of medium size, slightly longer than tall. Her color was more white than deep red. Her head had a slightly squarish appearance, with a deep dip between her eyes; her brows were prominent, her eyes almost round and neither bulging nor deep set. The lips were not pendulous or stretched, but tight to her teeth. The distance from nose to eyes was the same as from eyes to occiput, or top of the head. The ears hung low on the sides of the head, attached seemingly by roundish connections, and the hair hung about one and a half inches below the skin or ear proper, which dogmen call the leather. Belle's nose was moist, shining black, and quite prominent.

All of these head features blended into an expression of great attraction: they formed a dog which one would want very much to own—*very* much! The eyes alone seemed to say, "I trust you to be my friend!"

Belle's coat was straight but not coarse, with no trace of woolliness. Her ears did not snarl, but combed out as easily as a woman's hair. The coat was short along the front and sides of all four legs. The only long hair on the legs hung from their rear edge, and while it gave the impression of a luxuriant beauty, it was not sufficiently copious to become a mop and entrap filth. Indeed, the long hair did not reach the ground. The belly hair was the same texture and as easily combed. It fell like a fringe, which waved as she walked and augmented Belle's aristocratic beauty.

Pick her hind end up by the tail and drop her: her hind legs would land squarely under her with the line from hocks to ground perpendicular to the ground and just under the tip of her three-inch tail.

Raise her front end off the ground by lifting her by the chin: then drop her and those solid, strong front legs would also land squarely. Her whole side view made a solid, squarely rectangular picture, with her lovely head parallel to the ground.

But all this was the least important part about Belle. The Cocker Spaniel was developed, we are told, to be a hunting spaniel. So a true Cocker must be alert, eager, and must have an interest in anything that flies. Belle fulfilled all these requirements. She'd have made a great bird dog. But a proper Cocker is a retriever, which means, it goes without saying (although it must be said because the average layman doesn't know), that a retriever must have a "soft mouth." The retrieving dog won't

A full view of Idahurst Belle II. Wouldn't you love to own a dog like her?

bite, won't clamp down, and would find it exceedingly difficult to bite one's hand if he ever did take hold of it.

Belle could catch a baby chick, but wouldn't bite it. If she had, she would have been lacking one of the prime requisites of a Cocker Spaniel. Her ancestors certainly couldn't bite, for had one bitten retrieved birds it would have been destroyed. I once saw a friend, who had caught a lot of rats in an old French trap, releasing them one by one, his Cocker and his terrier chasing them. The Cocker caught the liberated rats as often as the terrier, but while the rat would be despatched with a quick crunch by the terrier, the Cocker carried those she caught and was severely bitten on the lips because she just couldn't crunch down on her live captive; such was she from selective breeding.

Belle's pups were like her. Idahurst Roderic, who sired more champions than any other Cocker in history in proportion to the number of bitches to which he was bred, was just that kind of dog.

Belle hungered for human companionship, yet when left in the kennel adapted herself admirably. She was a very easy keeper and lived on light rations, was never finicky, and was never allowed to grow fat. She wasn't in the least shy; she was friendly with those she knew, yet recognized a stranger. No matter how excited or frightened she became, she was never known to piddle; her bladder sphincter muscle never relaxed except when she willed it.

Friends, wouldn't you love to have a dog like Belle?

Well, that *was* the Cocker Spaniel, and that *can* be the Cocker Spaniel again. They weren't all like that, but so many were that the breed became more popular than any other in history.

Chapter 2

THIS IS THE COCKER

I sincerely hope that someday, perhaps ten or fifteen years from now, everything I have to say in this chapter could well be added to Chapter I, so that we can then say: "This *was* the Cocker Spaniel from 1940 to 1955." At the end of this book I want to talk about the Cocker's future.

Probably no group of persons on this green earth rationalize more than dog breeders. And no wonder; dogs can endear themselves to us much as do human beings, so that we find it hard to see their faults. Dog breeders fiercely resent another criticizing their dogs, even if the criticism is just. All this I know only too well. But I assume that you, the reader, wants both advice and the truth. So if I have to criticize, I shall.

Don't listen to those who say the Cocker is washed up as a breed. And don't believe those who say *any* Cocker is a perfect dog for you if you will only train him properly. You should know the following facts about the breed; they will guide you in acquiring a four-legged companion who will be a constant source of pleasure.

There's an interesting fact about Cockers: almost all of the typical ones—I mean of typical appearance—are registered in the American Kennel Club. The early breeders used only stock which was carefully controlled.

You don't find this state of affairs with all breeds. Farm Shepherds are seldom registered, and are bred to a standard of usefulness rather than appearance. Only one Hound in a hundred is registered, very few Spitz, very few American Fox Terriers, but Cocker Spaniels, regardless of their price, are nearly all recorded in the A.K.C. roster.

And this is well. The breeders of off-type dogs, those who don't care about quality in breeding, are less likely to register. Unfortunately many breeders of show-quality dogs have, because they are so easy to sell, bred for looks alone. And even the appearance, while still beautiful to certain show-minded people, has become in recent years one of the reasons for the rapid drop in popularity. Not the appearance of all Cockers, but just those few on the show circuits, and not all of them.

Breeder or Barber?

It was the New England Cocker Spaniel Club's annual banquet. I was sitting with Clarence Grey, one of the most respected of all Cocker judges, and one of the men most responsible for the dog's popularity, O. B. Gilman; another great breeder and the best-known Cocker breeder and exhibitor of all time, Herman Mellenthin. I was the speaker. My subject was "Heredity in the Cocker." About this time the hair on show Cockers was getting longer. I remember the conversation very vividly. Mr. Grey said, "What can a judge do today? There are practically two breeds of Cockers, the blacks and the non-blacks."

Mr. Gilman: "There shouldn't be, Clarence. If there are, you judges are making them that way."

Mr. Mellenthin: "O. B.'s right. If you didn't put the long-haired ones up, we wouldn't breed them that way. I can't win with a short-haired black." Then he asked me if there is any basic difference.

"Indeed there is," I answered. "Haven't you ever seen the long black hair on black-and-white dogs where the surrounding white hair is short? Sometimes the hair in these black patches will be five times as long as the white. I'm not sure whether the white is inhibited or whether there is something in the black hair follicles which makes for greater growth. That's why the all-black dog has naturally longer hair."

Mr. Grey: "Then the all-black is almost a different breed?"

"If you call one feature—length of hair—a basis for a breed," I told him.

Mr. Mellenthin: "It is in Dachshunds in Germany; they have the three kinds—wire, short, and long-haired breeds."

"Well," I said, "if Cocker breeders want two breeds, let them have them. On this basis it is possible."

Mr. Grey: "I believe it is coming to that."

Mr. Gilman: "Gentlemen, I've said before, and I can't be too emphatic about it—the first person to put an electric clipper on a Cocker will be the man to start the breed's downfall. Are Cocker people going to be breeders or barbers?"

Practically nobody believed Mr. Gilman when he preached his doctrine that the Cocker should be a natural dog, and that the only barbering permissible on a dog should be the removal of a few stray hairs with a razor-blade dresser or scissors. And so far as I can learn, the very person who was first to use an electric clipper was Bob MacGaughy, Mr. Gilman's kennel man. He set the style against his employer's policy and without his consent.

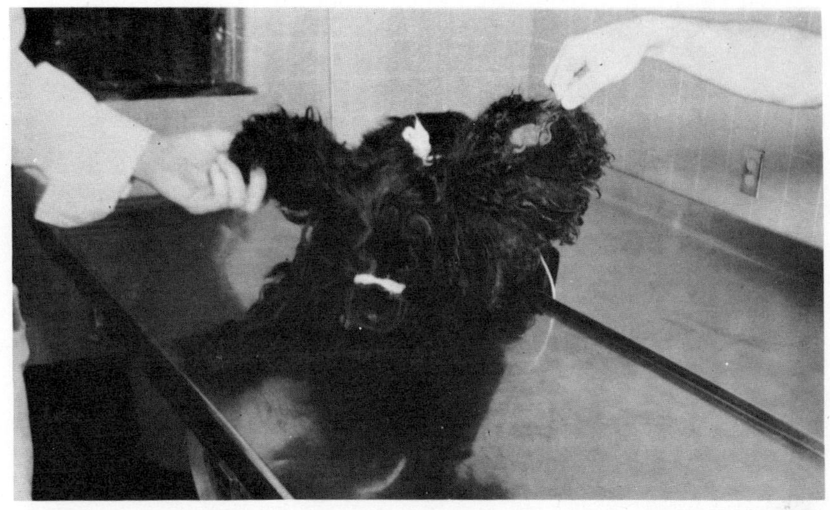

The average long haired or woolly Cocker soon accumulates enough foreign matter and objects in his ears to make combing impossible.

As the hair on all Cockers became longer and longer, as Cocker showmen became barbers as well as breeders, or bought great mops of black hair with a small dog inside and went to work with clippers and scissors, the breed increased rapidly and made O. B. Gilman's prophecy an apparent farce.

But was it? Once it passes out of puppyhood, a dog's natural life is about twelve years. Thousands of people bought Cockers expecting their dogs would be like Belle, or Flush in the movie *The Barretts of Wimpole Street,* or other natural dogs they knew and admired. Barbered black Cockers consistently won best-of-breed awards, and blacks are easier to breed. Prospective buyers looked at the beautifully groomed dogs in kennels and bought. Then their headaches began.

Year after year these Cocker owners paid to have the dogs clipped. Year after year the owner sighed a longer and more

Norma Shearer and friend in
"The Barretts of Wimpole Street"

tired sigh and finally admitted, "I wish someone had told me it would be all this trouble. My next dog will be short haired." And the next dog is short haired. And this is one of the principal reasons for the Cocker's decline.

The kennel owner may deny this, but he is not in the position of the man who does the clipping or the veterinarian who treats skin diseases on such dogs. Well knowing the dog will be clipped, the owner stops all grooming several months before clipping time. Then he takes the dog to the clipper at a boarding kennel or veterinary establishment and says, "Give him a *comfort clip.*" The comfort on the owners' minds is really their own as well as the dogs'. "Sure he looks awful," they say, "but he's comfortable, and so will I be till that mop grows in again."

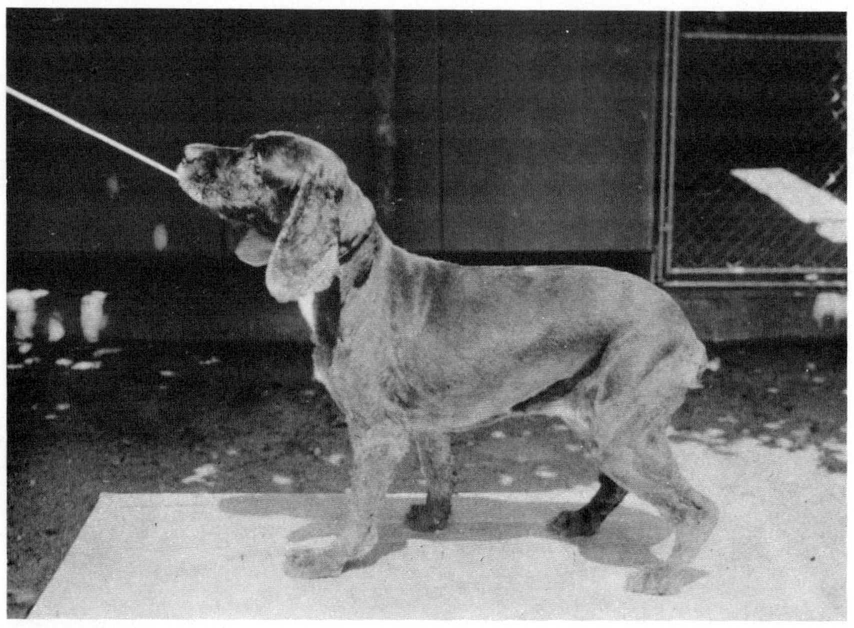

This is a "comfort clip" which is entirely unnecessary in Cockers with proper coats.

Does the veterinarian advise his clients to buy Cockers? He advises against it. Who, in his right mind, would advise anyone to buy himself a load of trouble? The fact is that even though at least half of the present-day Cockers do not need a lot of care, the disgraceful coats on so many tar all Cockers with the same brush. Today, because of the clipping fetish, even cream-colored Cockers are being shown with immense coats.

And it is not only the long coat, but the woolly one, which

debases the breed. If you want to see what the dog really is, you must see it in its natural state; the clipped dog is only part of it. The pictures illustrate the true Cocker Spaniel of the barbering show people. Contrast them with the kind of Cocker which made the breed famous.

And so I advise you who are interested in the breed to refuse to buy any unnatural Cocker. There are thousands of wonder-

Here is a natural unclipped but otherwise well cared for dog of the woolly type.

ful natural dogs to choose from. If you will insist on seeing the parent dogs in their natural state, and you realize that their puppies will tend to be like them, you will be doing yourself and the breed a real service.

Veterinarians can give an excellent estimate of the dogs they treat. If a Cocker puppy screams shrilly from the mere prick of a hypodermic needle, if he struggles and wets; if a mature dog snaps when having his temperature taken or his teeth examined, such dogs just aren't fit for breeders, even in the hope that something good will come out of them. While veterinarians can't deprecate their clients' dogs, they can tell them which dogs behave as sound dogs should.

Before buying a puppy, the author advises, look at the parents for their appearance will give you an idea of what the pup will grow to be. Do you want a Cocker like this with all the care which it entails?

And don't believe those who say that all dogs have sound temperaments, and that training is entirely to blame for unsociable traits. In an as-yet-unreported study I made, a record was kept of puppy behavior at the time of vaccination. With all conditions as nearly the same as was possible to make them, some puppies squealed, some stood stoically, some struggled, urinated, and defecated. None had been previously vaccinated or injected in any way, yet one finds these early differences, which run in strains.

Beauty? Brains? Or both?

At that same meeting in Boston when the four of us dined together, one of the speakers talked about size in Cockers. The

Field Trial Champion Blue Waters Magnificent retrieves a pheasant.

show standard put the upper limit at 28 pounds. Beyond this a Cocker should have been disqualified. "You can't show a 15-inch Beagle in the 13-inch class," our speaker pointed out. "The upper limit is too small. The Cocker is a bird dog, and at 28 pounds he is too small to carry a grouse in his little mouth." Everybody agreed the dog was a bird dog and that he needed a bird dog's attributes, but few agreed that a dog needed to be over 28 pounds to carry a bird. I want here to discuss the mental characteristics of a real Cocker, but, in passing, isn't it laughable to hear people tell us that Cockers are bird dogs, and then to watch those same persons show oversized Cockers with so much long, woolly hair all but dragging the ground that if such a dog were hunted he would become so snarled in brush that he might well be stuck there and die of thirst? Or, if he weren't caught in briars, he would become so loaded with sticks, filth, and burrs that he couldn't work any more.

And who wants a black dog, anyway, to hunt with? Pointer and Setter men want all the white they can get on dogs, to be able to see them with ease. How far can rationalization go?

Today, while there are thousands of Cockers left with perfect dispositions, there are thousands more whose temperaments are such that they would be better off dead. Here again one sees the patient Cocker owner whose dog has became endeared to him by propinquity, not by disposition, who won't dispose of the dog. How he sighs when death finally takes a creature so obnoxious to others! The moral is: if you're going to own a dog at all, seek until you find one with a reliable disposition.

Very likely many bad-dispositioned dogs were ruined by their owners, but proper Cockers won't bite and can be easily trained. Couple a nasty disposition with a big thick coat, and what have you? Something only a mother could love—and the mother in this case is the doting, spoiling owner.

Today even I, who have handled thousands of dogs of all breeds, bad, good, and wonderful, and think I can handle any regardless of disposition, look with suspicion on every Cocker presented for examination or treatment, until I get to know the dog. Instinctively I reach for a roll of tape to tie the dog's mouth, frequently insulting both dog and owner. But if you have been burned by touching one stove which you didn't know was hot, you are instinctively careful about all stoves. If you've been burned by half the stoves you touched, you're conditioned mighty well.

That is why almost all veterinarians approach all Cockers new to them very gingerly. Some I know insist that all Cocker owners place their dogs on the examining table; the doctor fears the dogs' bites. All this was a revelation to me when I first began to practice in 1941. I had had as many as 75 grown Cockers used in nutritional work, and would no more have had a second's hesitation about picking one up than I would in kissing my wife; handling a Cocker was pleasant to me. My dogs just didn't know they had teeth to bite with. How different these carelessly bred dogs I am now called upon to treat!

I see why all this vast change has occurred. There was one very famous show dog so vicious that only one handler could touch him. (Once he bit a judge, who didn't disqualify the dog.) I must have seen a dozen of this dog's progeny which were plain nasty, even biting their owners, who foolishly kept them. The temperament was inherited, though not necessarily in any Mendelian manner. It was so obvious that even in competent hands this kind of un-Cockerly disposition showed itself in such a way that it must have been hereditary: it should have been patent to all that regardless of show quality the miscreant should have been incarcerated, just as are human beings whose heredity and training make them unfit for human society.

But no, champion Cockers became the sires of many Cockers! And I happen to know that, in several cases, it was not economic necessity that prompted the use of unsuitable dogs, but rather the desire for self-glorification, for several vicious show champions used for breeding were owned by very wealthy people.

Most show dogs are show dogs only. The owners usually

know nothing about them except that the dogs show well and are formed and barbered in such a way that they win. Of course we want dogs conforming to a standard, but that is only 10 per cent of the value of a dog to a one-dog owner: he or she buys a dog for its temperament. How does the show-dog owner know whether the dog has competence as a hunter, the perfect Cocker disposition, or a soft mouth? He often doesn't. But he had better start learning, and thus help bring the Cocker again up to the predominant place he deserves in the world of dogs.

Before you buy a Cocker, insist on seeing its parents. Push them around, handle them; see if you can make one reveal a tendency to nip. And watch the pup; maul it, examine it for early tendency to shyness. There are thousands of marvelously sound Cocker temperaments. Cockers are not so easily sold as they were, and if you will insist on a sound pup you will be doing both yourself and the breeder a favor. For yourself, you will get twelve years or more of wondrous companionship; you will also show the breeder that it doesn't pay to raise treacherous dogs.

The Piddling Tendency

We have discussed two Cocker characteristics that need to be eliminated from the breed, but there is a third that has militated against the Cocker's continuing popularity fully as much as, if not more than, the long woolly coat and the tendency to bite. This is the weakness of a small muscle that encircles the neck of the bladder, known as a *sphincter*. It is this muscle and its nervous control that holds back the urine. In the cases of at least a third of present-day Cockers, if you bend over one to lift it, the dog squats and leaves a puddle on the floor. In the case of some, mere excitement relaxes the muscle, and the dog piddles.

Some owners excuse this degenerate characteristic on the basis of cuteness. It often persists throughout the dog's life, and it is both hereditary and to some degree due to training, but you don't need to buy a puppy with this trait, which manifests itself generally at a very early age. This defect occurs in many breeds besides the Cocker.

Piddling Cockers ruin floors, rugs, clothing. It is necessary to keep sponges or mops handy as part of such dogs' equipment. The majority of present-day Cockers have sound bladder sphincters. *When choosing your pup, have the seller put a newspaper on the floor, set the puppy down on it, then bend over it, pick it up, and look at the paper. If there is even a drop of urine on it, that's not the pup for you.*

You will hear a great deal about how "money breeders" are responsible for the slump in Cockers. Breeding kennel owners who wanted dogs easiest to sell did breed and sell inferior specimens. But substantial breeders, who have the breed's real interest at heart, will tell you that the recent loss of popularity is smoking out the money breeders and eliminating them.

But when they are gone, their disappearance by itself won't return the breed to popularity. It is fully as necessary to get rid of the mops of hair and inferior dispositions in the dogs kept by show people. It's just as important to select for brains as for looks, and you can force this kind of selection if you will buy puppies only from dogs that show vivacity, intelligence, and all the qualities you want in a canine companion, because to a great degree it is *"like sire and dam, like pups,"* and not "like father, like son," as the familiar adage goes.

This, then, is the Cocker Spaniel: a breed composed of thou-

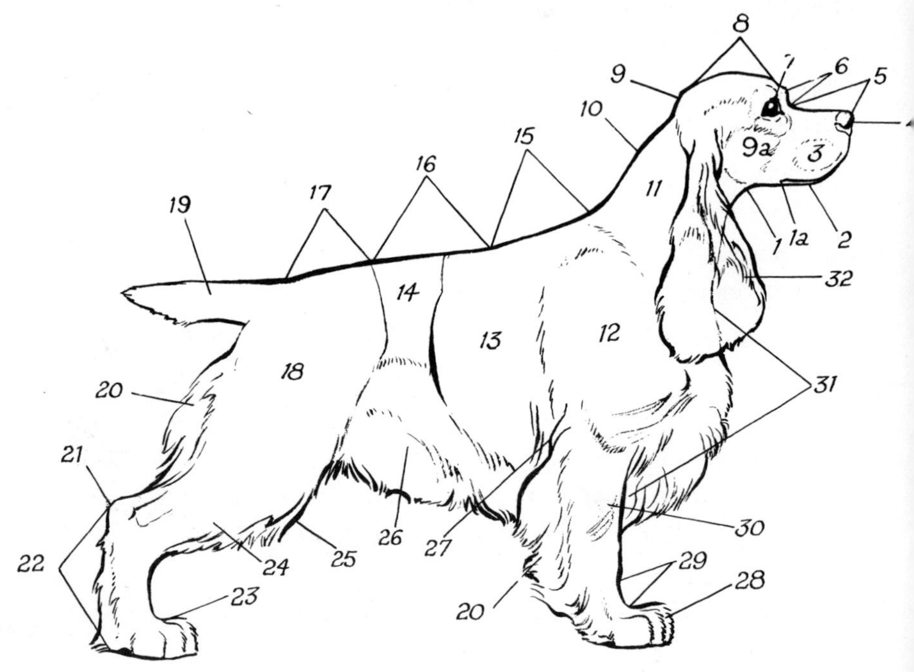

PARTS OF THE COCKER

1. Throat. 1A. Lip corner (flew). 2. Under jaw. 3. Muzzle. 4. Nose. 5. Foreface. 6. Stop. 7. Eye. 8. Skull. 9. Occiput. 9A. Cheek. 10. Crest (of neck). 11. Neck. 12. Shoulders. 13. Ribbing. 14. Loin. 15. Withers. 16. Back. 17. Croup. 18. Thigh (Quarter, haunch). 19. Tail. 20. Feathering. 21. Point of hock. 22. Hock (Metatarsus). 23. Foot. 24. Lower thigh. 25. Stifle. 26. Abdomen. 27. Elbow. 28. Foot. 29. Pastern. 30. Forearm. 31. Forechest. 32. Ear (leather).

sands of grand, adaptable little dogs, but also of a lot of inferior specimens that need to be eliminated from the breed. The inferior dogs are those which, besides not conforming to the Cocker standard (which, by the way, says "legs well feathered," and feathering is the hair behind the legs, not beside them), have too much coat, untrustworthy dispositions, and too little

Faulty Heads

A. Too short in muzzle. Dish faced. Domed skull. Eye haw.

B. Occiput not strongly defined. Stop not sharp enough. Roman nose. Heavy flews. Muzzle not square or deep enough. Ears too short, set too high, too thick at attachment to skull.

control of their bladder sphincters. Be sure yours has none of these faults.

Here is the A.K.C. standard, to help you know how an ideal Cocker should look:

Skull.—Not so heavy as in other Sporting Spaniels, with

smooth forehead and clearly defined eyebrows and stop, the median line distinctly marked and gradually disappearing until lost rather more than halfway up, a well-developed, rounded, and comparatively wide skull showing no prominence in the cheeks, which, like the side of the muzzle, should present a smooth, clean-cut appearance.

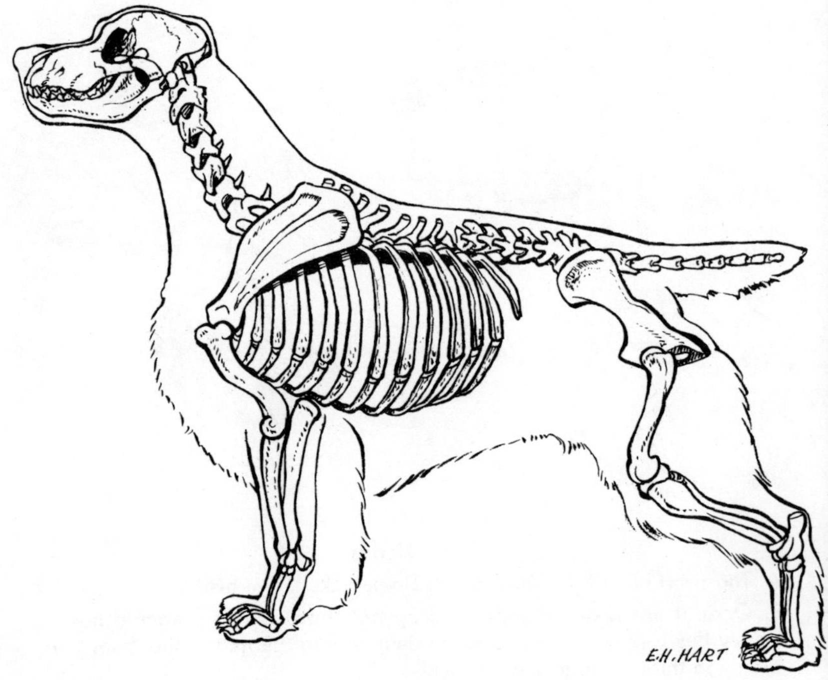

Skeletal Structure

Muzzle.—Proportionately shorter and lighter than in the Field Spaniel, showing no fullness under the eyes, the jaws even and approaching squareness. Teeth sound and regular, the front ones meeting. Lips cut off square, preventing any appearance of snipiness. Nose well developed in all directions and black in color excepting in the reds, livers, parti-colors of these shades and in the roans of the lighter lines, when it may be brown or black.

Eyes.—Comparatively large, round, rather full, yet never goggled nor weak, as in the Toy Spaniel kind. They should be dark in the blacks, black and tans, the darker shades of parti-colors, and roans. In the reds and livers and in the parti-colors and roans of these colors they should be brown, but of a shade not lighter than hazel.

Ears.—Lobular, set low, leather fine, and not extending beyond the nose; well clothed with long, silky hair, which should

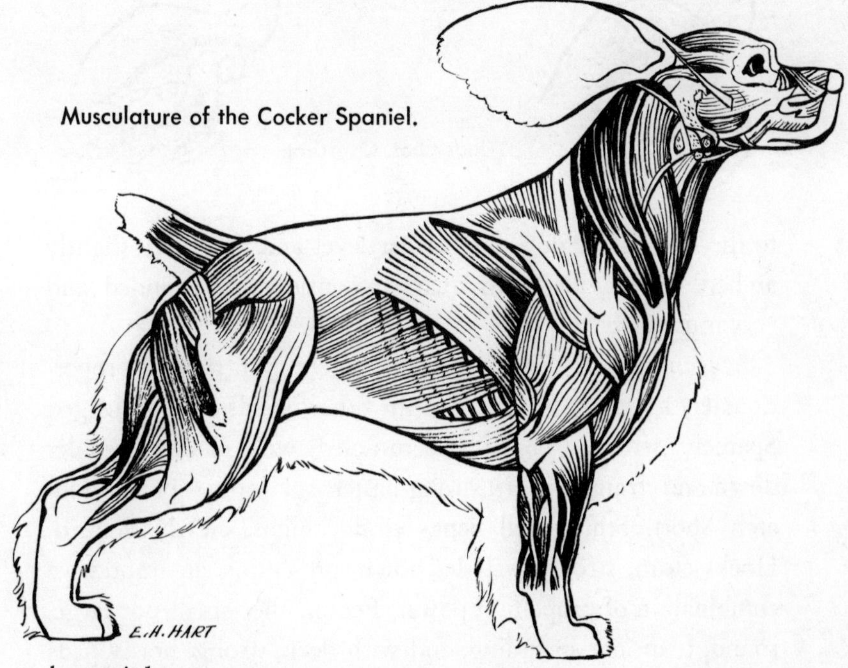

Musculature of the Cocker Spaniel.

be straight or wavy.

Neck and Shoulders.—Neck sufficiently long to allow the nose to reach the ground easily, muscular, free from throatiness, and running into clean-cut, sloping shoulders, which should not be wide at the points.

Body.—Comparatively short, compact, and firmly knit together, giving the impression of a concentration of power and untiring activity. Chest deep rather than wide, not narrow fronted nor yet so wide as to interfere with free action of the forelegs. Ribs well sprung, deep and carried far back, short in the couplings and flank, free from any tucked appearance. Back and loin immensely strong and compact in proportion

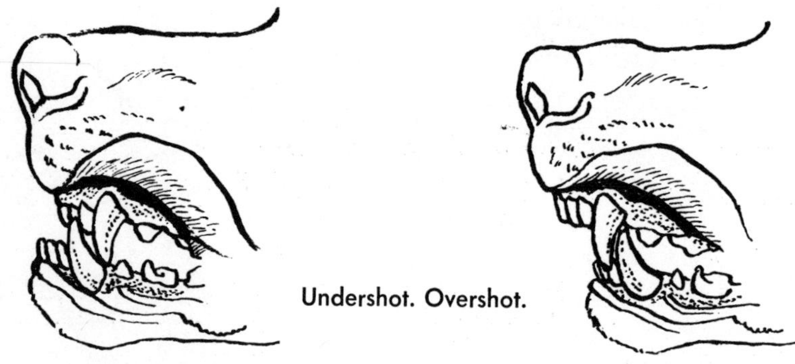

Undershot. Overshot.

to the size of the dog, the former level and the latter slightly arched. Hips wide, with quarters considerably rounded and very muscular.

Legs and Feet.—Forelegs short and straight, though proportionately longer than in any of the other breeds of short-legged Spaniels; strongly boned and muscled, with elbows well let down and straight, short, strong pasterns. Hindlegs proportionately short. Stifles well bent, strong thighs, clearly defined. Hocks clean, strong, well let down, presenting an impressive combination of propelling power. Feet neither small nor large, round, firm, not spreading, and with deep, strong, horny pads and plenty of hair between the toes. They should turn neither in nor out.

STRUCTURAL FAULTS

1. Hind legs lack angulation. Wet throat. Short neck. Tail too long and set too low. Not enough angulation in shoulder. Soft in pastern. Croup too rounded. Sway back. Too leggy.

2. Roach back. Mutton withers (too flat). Tail too short. Legs too short. Loin too long. Hare foot. Angulation too extreme in hind quarters.

Cocker Fronts

a. Excellent. b. Too narrow. Feet east and west. c. Loaded shoulder. Out at elbow.

Stern.—Should be set on and carried level with the back, and when at work its action should be incessant in this, the brightest and merriest of the whole Spaniel family.

Cocker Rears

a. Excellent. b. Cowhocked and dewclaws.

Coat.—Flat or slightly waved, silky and very dense, with ample Setter-like feather.

Color and Markings.—Blacks should be jet black, and reds.

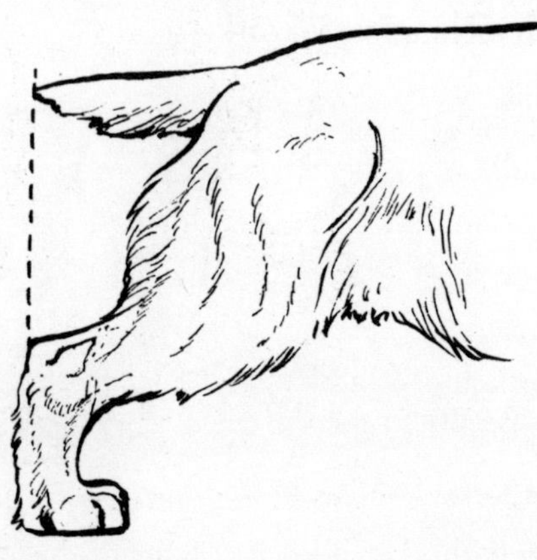

livers, etc., should never be faded or "washy" shades, but of good, sound colors. White on the chest of self-colors, while objectionable, should not disqualify.

Weight.—Not under 18 nor exceeding 24 pounds.

General Description.—Embodying the foregoing, i.e., a neat headed, wide-awake, serviceable-looking little dog, with an expression of great intelligence; short in body when viewed from above, yet standing over considerable ground for one of his inches upon strong, straight front legs, with wide, muscular quarters suggestive of immense power, especially when viewed from behind. A downward tendency in front he ought not to possess, but should stand well up at the shoulders, like the clever little sporting dog that he is. Massive in appearance by reason of his sturdy body, powerful quarters, and strong, well-boned limbs, he should, nevertheless, impress one as being a dog capable of considerable speed combined with great powers of endurance and in all his movements he should be quick and merry, with an air of alertness and a carriage of head and stern suggestive of an inclination to work.

	Points
Skull	8
Muzzle	10
Eyes	7
Ears	4
Neck and shoulders	15
Body	18
Legs and feet	18
Stern	5
Coat	10
Color and marking	5
Total	100

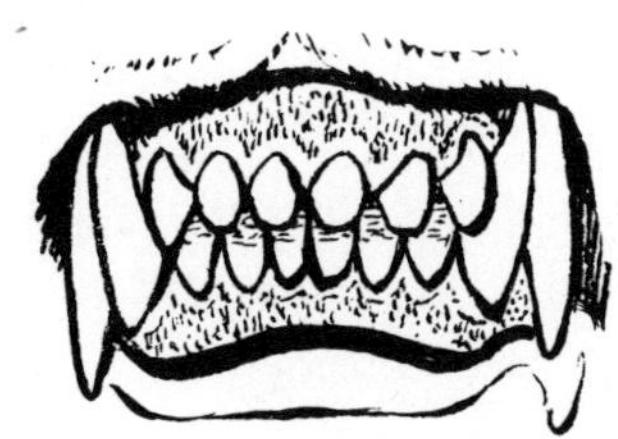

Proper scissors bite (from front).

Chapter 3

THREE TYPES OF COCKER

Today we find three types of Cockers, all descended from the old Obo type in England. These early English dogs, as every Cocker breeder knows, were a bird-hunting type. The three kinds are: the true American Cocker, which is still amazingly like the old type; the newfangled, long-haired, highly barbered show type which is rapidly making the breed unpopular, partly because of its unsanitary aspects but more especially the enormous care it requires. Third is the popular modern English type, recognized by the American Kennel Club as a breed distinct from the American. The diagram shows the differences between the three quite accurately.

To go back to the conversation related in the last chapter, when Clarence Grey suggested that the Cocker was developing into two distinct types on the basis of hair length, this great Cocker judge, I believe, was right—for we do definitely today

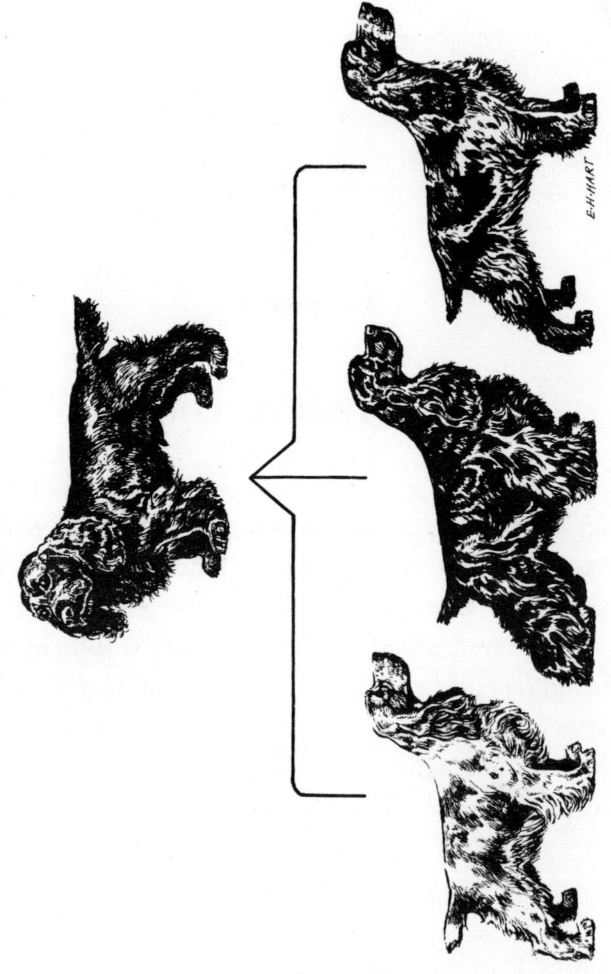
ORIGINAL OBO TYPE COCKER AND THE THREE PRESENT DAY TYPES WHICH STEMMED FROM OBO TYPE.
E.H. HART
1. American Cocker.
2. Woolly Cocker.
3. English Cocker.

have two types of American Cocker. Then why not have *two breeds* based on this difference? One breed the American; the other the Woolly Cocker. No one can fail to admire the great beauty of the latter, and the loving, painstaking care that went

This magnificent Best-in-Show winner at the 1954 Westminster Kennel Club's show at Madison Square Garden is a show man's dream. The public appreciates the enormous amount of care and grooming which produced him. International News Pictures.

into breeding and barbering it into the dog we see in the shows. If a class of breeders want it, let them have it, but we must not let the public, which largely does not want that kind, think it represents the true Cocker. Yes, make it a different breed!

Anyone can see how well the American dog has kept to the type and how the Woolly Cocker breeders have veered off one way while the English have veered another.

The English dog is reasonably short haired, with only feathering on the legs and the rest of the leg hair short. It is a larger breed, much longer in the head, and without the marked stop of the American.

As they stand today, at least judging by those I have seen, only one English in dozens possesses an unreliable temperament. English dogs are excellent hunters, too, but the long, almost-Collie head does not endow them with that appealing expression which is one of the most endearing features of the old-type American. In form, the English have moved further away from the original than have the American. Whether this is any advantage can be debated. The proponents claim that the longer jaw gives the dogs greater ability to retrieve a pheasant. The American dogs seem to do it ably, if with a little more trouble. But for Hungarians, quail or woodcock, the longer jaws are no advantage.

Best English Cocker at Madison Square Garden's 71st annual show. Ch. Corner Boy of Ware is ably shown by Virginia Tuck Nichols, author of *Show Your Own Dog.*

The fact that our English cousins have been so careful to destroy the dogs with unreliable dispositions, even while the Cocker was going to the head of all their dogs in popularity, speaks well for the breeders, and makes us rather ashamed that our own Cocker breeders should have been so remiss.

The fetish for breeding too much coat has even affected some English Cockers. Except for his ears, it would be hard to fault this dog as a companion.

The Woolly Cocker is an American dog with a prodigious crop of hair that needs constant barbering and combing. He is a dog for only a select few—for those who have time on their hands and not much else to do.

The dog needs extra-special environmental conditions. He must be kept away from any straw, bedding, sawdust, dirt, sticks, twigs, or leaves. He must be cared for far more methodically and industriously than a Poodle, because the hair which is allowed to remain on him is on his legs, chest, and the underside of his body, while the Poodle's long hair is kept off his feet and permitted to grow on the body.

Probably no more filthy type of dog exists, from the viewpoint of the homeowner, than a modern Woolly Cocker. He is useless for the country place, and is strictly a city or apartment dog, preferably for those with wealth, who can afford to have him barbered and groomed by professionals.

The Woolly Cocker is useless, too, for the hunter, because few hunters want a dog which must be constantly combed. A shorthaired dog, such as the Pointer, is sometimes preferred even to a Setter. And Setters are really easy dogs to care for, because they possess no woolly undercoat to tangle with the feather, belly, and chest hair. Having groomed hundreds of Setters and thousands of Cockers, I know that just about the only trouble one finds in grooming them is in the American Cocker—a tendency to mat under the ears and behind the hind legs, but these mats may be clipped out without defacing the dog.

The Woolly Cocker is the showman's dog *par excellence*. Where the American Cocker's defects are obvious, the showman can cover them completely with hair. Then, if there is no angulation in the hind legs, that fact can't be detected. If the feet are flat, they never show. If there is insufficient stop above the eyes, the hair is clipped so the crew cut looks any height the showman wants it, giving the appearance of a high brow. Even the gait is hard to fault, because all the judge sees is a lot of hair waving about.

If you observe the show poses of all Woolly Cockers, you find them straight-legged in front, but behind the legs are stretched out so that the dogs appear like hackney horses—in no way corresponding with the Cocker standard, which states that the hind legs, from hocks down, must be perpendicular to the ground.

There will be those who say that all of us who are opposed to barbering Cockers are reactionaries; that the new look represents progress; why should the breed stand still?

The answer obviously is that breeders who want woolly coats want the easiest thing. This is not progress but deterioration or degeneration. It is easy enough to hire experts to barber but it is a real feat to breed natural dogs toward perfection. And the lack of public acceptance of the ultra-long haired and the woolly types should have long ago been warning that these types were harming our wonderful Cocker.

The real Cocker—the kind that Idahurst Belle and thousands of others exemplified, and the kind that will again be bred to put the breed on top—is free from all the objectionable features of the Woolly type, and the heads have that wonderfully appealing expression not possessed in so high a degree by any other breed, and certainly not by the English, fine as that breed is in all other respects.

If you are a prospective purchaser of a Cocker, or are considering taking up the breeding of Cockers as a hobby, you will be interested in the relative expense of maintaining the three types. The American and the English can easily be groomed at no cost except for the purchase of a comb, a pair of barber's scissors, and a Duplex trimmer, or one of similar design. The feet may be trimmed a little if you wish, and combing once every week or two is enough unless your dog's ears become tangled in burrs, which can quite easily be combed out. Any unruly hairs that refuse to lie flat can be removed simply with the razor-blade-type dresser.

The Woolly type will need to be clipped at least six times a year, if it is to be kept looking like the show prototype. This includes clipping around the feet, too.

Combing is the big job. Once a day is none too often to comb your dog if he is to be kept in tiptop condition. If he does get

If you do not keep the woolly Cocker's coat trimmed this is what it grows to look like. This, then, not the trimmed specimen, *is* the woolly Cocker.

loose in the country, you may have to spend an hour removing the foreign material from his leg hair. Should he get into a brook and then in mud—and if he is a typical Cocker he will love to—you have a bath to give him, as you would the other types, but on top of that you have a drying, a combing, and an untangling job which may take you another hour or two.

Should the Woolly Cocker have an unreliable disposition, it

is better to give sedative pills, which your veterinarian can supply you, because combing may involve a lot of tugging and pain for the dog. We have quite a few dogs of this type to groom, and we invariably anesthetize them at the owner's request, so they will not have to "go through so much torture." Eventually they are given comfort clips to spare the owner's

A cross bred Cocker x Wire Haired Fox Terrier. By inbreeding such dogs a Wire Haired Cocker could easily be produced—that is, if still another type of Cocker is desirable.

having to comb them, with the consequent risk of being bitten.

If you calculate your own time, or figure, what you pay a professional to clip such a dog, you will find it can run, to at least a hundred dollars a year.

There is another type of hair one sees in small quantities on some well bred Cockers which is akin to the wire hair of terriers.

This characteristic could easily be developed by selection to produce a wire haired dog much like the wire haired Dachshund. Up to now this wiry hair has been trimmed off and few persons have seen it. If a wire haired type is ever desired, crosses with wire haired Fox Terriers could more quickly establish such a breed. The illustration shows such a cross before trimming or plucking. I have seen dozens of them. Their coats are less trouble to care for than the woolly coats.

This bas-relief contains the ideas of many breeders and judges and was made at the height of the Cocker's popularity.

Chapter 4

YOUR COCKER'S ENVIRONMENT

The Cocker Spaniel is such an adaptable creature that he accommodates himself to all sorts of human and canine environments. I am thinking of many supremely happy Cockers I've known: one lived in a third-floor hall bedroom with his owner, who took him for walks morning and evening, on the New Haven Green. Another was kept in a cellar apartment, and I recall all sorts of environments between these and the wide-open spaces of extensive estates where other Cockers romped. And they were all happy.

If there ever was a dog demanding a minimum of fancy environment and pampering, the Cocker is that dog. I should know from my own studies. I've raised several hundred in wire-bottomed pens like those shown on page 54, and hundreds more in 10 x 20 foot runs like those shown on page 50. There just isn't any *one way* to keep Cockers. They can stand cold and heat better than many other breeds: they are tough. For years I raised all my dogs, Cockers included, in outdoor pens and coops without heat, right through the winter, and they looked and seemed to feel better than dogs that were pampered in heated kennels. The houses were accommodated to the size

Some of the author's Cockers were kept in runs 10 by 20 feet with hutches attached. The dogs furnished their own heat in winter but deep bedding was used in their houses.

of the dog, so that the pups or grown dogs had a minimum of space to heat. Many a cold night pups tore the burlap door coverings off and, with the temperature 10° above zero, came out in the morning, their breaths almost white against the bitterly cold air, stretched, trotted across the snow to their food pans, gobbled up the last morsel, and then ate snow or ice for their water.

This wasn't cruel to the little dogs. I used to envy them their remarkable ability to adapt so admirably to the cold.

When I went to Auburn, Alabama, to earn my D.V.M., I had a lot of my Cockers sent to me. There, where the heat was about as intense as in any part of the United States, those won-

More of the author's Cockers, happy and healthy and kept in the open.

derful rascals tossed it off as effortlessly as they had the Connecticut cold.

No, you need not pamper your Cockers. Lest you have any idea that one must have a certain climate to keep one or breed many, look in any dog magazine and see Cockers advertised from every state in the United States, and Mexico and Canada as well.

One finds champions coming from the most inexpensive barrel kennels as well as from plush kennels where every luxury known to dogdom's owners in lavished. Kennels could hardly have been plainer than some which have raised more than two dozen champions, nor more luxurious than the Idahurst at Dedham, yet each produced approximately the same number of outstanding dogs.

So, if you keep your Cocker inside, give him an old pillow, a piece of carpet, or a fancy frame bed, but no wicker basket, or he will chew it to pieces and may swallow enough to harm his digestive tract. He'll appreciate any bed you give him, and if you're not careful you'll find him sleeping on yours.

If you must keep him out-of-doors, and you live where it gets cold in the winter, be sure his shelter is as small as is comfortable for him, so his body won't have to heat too much space. Keep deep straw bedding under him, with a high-grade flea powder sprinkled in the straw each time it is changed.

Don't keep him on a concrete run or he will wear out his elbows, and, too, you'll have trouble keeping him free of worms. A sand run, from which you hoe the stools on to a shovel once a day, is most sanitary. Should the run become worm infested, you can shovel off a few inches of sand and replace it with fresh. Use clean screened sand, not gravel or cinders.

The same suggestion applies to the kenneling of breeding dogs. The sand will have to be changed more often. Don't try to keep too many in one run: four in a 10 x 20 foot run is maximum. Cockers, while kind to us and having soft mouths with retrieved objects, can use their teeth on one another when necessary. Although it is never admitted publicly, several of the top Cockers of all time have been killed by pen mates ganging up on them, much as if the attentions given these champions were resented.

No better plan for puppy rearing has yet been devised than the wire-bottomed pen. In many kennels it is now standard equipment. The illustrations show one in process of construc-

Steps in the construction of a wire bottom pen.

tion. My early pens (I pioneered them) were made with ½-inch mesh bottoms and 1½-inch fox netting for the remainder. It was soon obvious that the ½-inch mesh was neither large enough nor strong enough, and all subsequent pens have been made of No. 9 gauge, 1-inch mesh wire. Most of the soft puppy stools drop through it, and any of the firmer ones which do not can easily be pushed through with a stiff brush and the netting washed at the same time.

The sides and top are made of heaviest turkey netting, the

meshes of which are 1 x 2 inches. This makes the most nearly perfect pen I have ever seen, strong and solid in every dimension. Puppies' feet develop beautifully on wire, one toe often bearing much of the weight, so that the aggregate of strengthened toes makes excellent feet. The nails need more frequent trimming than those of Cockers raised on sand.

A battery of wire bottom pens. These make an ideal arrangement for raising puppies.

It is a good idea to let the dogs out for romps once a day, but this is not essential for their development. I have had mine trained to race about in a large run but to trot home to their pens at mealtime.

While this method of raising Cockers is both excellent and adaptable to a back yard, most people who have never tried it will want to provide larger quarters. A house large enough for four grown Cockers is shown in the illustration. So long as the hutch space is not too large, the dogs may be kept outside in winter as well as summer. The platform is excellent for sunning on cold, bright days and should face south. Being raised

Cocker puppies raised on wire have excellent feet because each toe may bear the weight of the puppy and the whole foot is thus made strong.

off the ground, the house keeps cleaner and less sand will be tracked inside.

The regular kennel house is easiest to care for in bad weather. Kennel men prefer it, yet diseases spread in a kennel faster than in places where dogs are kept in runs several yards apart. However, with modern protective methods there is less chance of infection than there once was, and the indoor kennel is consequently safer, especially in the case of the several diseases of the distemper complex.

When one is a poor trainer and unable to control barking in one's dogs, and it is desired to raise Cockers close to neighbors, then a tight, soundproof kennel, in which the dogs can be shut,

Doghouses with verandas large enough for four mature Cockers. This pen with four houses is excellent for keeping bitches in when they whelp during warm weather.

is essential. Among these no single one is best. If you visit half-a-dozen Cocker breeders and ask for suggestions, you will learn from the owners varying ideas and improvements for any kind and come away with the best plan for your needs and circumstances.

Chapter 5

YOUR COCKER'S FOOD

I could tell you in one short paragraph how to feed a Cocker, or a whole kennel full, but dog owners want to know why, hence a whole chapter.

There are as many ways to feed dogs as there are dogs. There is no one best way, since local conditions vary greatly, and certain foods are available to some and not to others. In my book *Feeding Our Dogs* I have a long list of widely differing but successful methods of dog feeding. And the differences are amazing in their scope.

We are told that the natural food of cats and dogs consists of rodents, such as mice or rabbits. But wouldn't a cat owner look suspicious if he spent part of a day trapping mice to feed his cat! Wolves, the probable ancestors of dogs, besides eating rodents, killed larger species and ate the stomach and intestinal contents as well as the muscular meat. But who is going to the slaughterhouse to buy stomach contents for his dog and add them to muscular meat? Once I did feed about five tons of this in research, but I didn't smell like honeysuckle each time the mixing was over. Yes, the dogs liked it. My wife didn't. The idea was impractical.

So you and I, being sensible, realize we can't offer our dogs

Scioto Sand Storm—an excellent Ohio dog.

their natural food, so we try to approximate it and fulfill all their nutritional requirements. How can we best do it?

Protein. This important dietary essential may be supplied by feeding meat, fish, milk, cheese, or vegetable matter of high-protein content, such as soy bean meal. We can use these ingredients fresh, frozen, or dried. If they are dried, they will be better preserved by the vacuum process, which dries at temperatures well below the boiling point, thus removing only water and doing almost no harm to proteins or vitamins.

Carbohydrates. If we take bitches' milk as a guide to an ideal ration, we find it is composed of about 29 per cent protein, 13 per cent carbohydrate, and 43 per cent fat. If we take a whole woodchuck as another guide, we find the carbohydrate con-

Sporter Nebio—one of the taller Cockers of his time.

siderably higher because of the stomach contents, and the fat about 30 per cent. Research has shown that a diet with 50 per cent carbohydrate is satisfactory (on a dry basis, of course).

Carbohydrates may be supplied as starches and sugars. Some dog biscuits contain 85 per cent baked starch. Baking turns starch into dextrin, which tastes sweet, and dogs like it. Syrups are fed in fairly large quantities to dogs in the form of sweetening in corn flakes. There is plenty of starch-digesting enzyme, to handle even more starch, in the fluids discharged into dogs' intestines; but when too much is fed, the protein percentage naturally goes down as the carbohydrate rises.

Fat. If more than 25 per cent (on a dry basis) of a sedentary dog's diet is fat, his excretions will be too soft. A hunting Cocker can handle 40 per cent fat while he is exercising hard.

Fat may be fed as suet, lard, lamb, fish, chicken, and bacon fats, or even vegetable shortening. The dog uses it, deposits the unnecessary unused part in his tissues as adipose and, in time, turns this fat into dog fat. From each unit of fat he gets two and one quarter times as much energy as he does when his body burns protein and carbohydrate. So the use of fat is one way to save money feeding dogs. At 1955 prices, fat costs about 5 cents a pound at any butcher's. If dry dog food costs 12 cents a pound, then fat is actually worth 30 cents. Too bad we can't feed over 25 per cent in the ration!

Fat has valuable nutritional qualities. The fat-soluble vitamins are stored in body fat. Sometimes beef suet is actually yellow from vitamin A. Puppies, but not grown dogs, require vitamin E, and if a lactating bitch is fed plenty of fat, the puppies will get it in this way as well as from grains.

Then, too, fat insures better digestion of other foods because in some way it causes the dog's food to pass more slowly through his intestines. It also spares vitamins of the B-complex, possibly because of greater bacterial activity within the dog's intestines.

And fat, because it is so easily assimilated, produces a plump appearance in dogs and growing puppies.

Calories. While they are not an ingredient of food, we must take heat units represented by calories into consideration, in order to know how much food a Cocker requires. These hardy little fellows will almost all eat at least 30 per cent more than they need for daily requirements, and some 50 per cent. A well-fed Cocker is always hungry enough to snatch and eat avidly a crust of bread from one's hand. Because they are such "easy keepers," as the stockman says, one must always be watching them for their tendency to become overweight. Some people call them gluttons—really a highly complimentary term, because it must be realized that no normal Cocker ever needs pampering to get it to eat. A Cocker that is not hungry is either sick or "spoiled rotten."

Here are the amounts I have found mature Cockers of various weights require to maintain weight under kennel conditions:

TABLE I

Pounds	*Calorie Requirement*	*Canned Food*	*Dry Food*	*Beef*	*Eggs (average size)*	*Fat*	*Dog Biscuits*
18	600	1 lb. 8 oz.	6 oz.	12 oz.	6	2½ oz.	6 oz.
20	650	1 lb. 10 oz.	6½ oz.	13 oz.	6–7	2½ oz.	6½ oz.
22	700	1 lb. 12 oz.	7 oz.	14 oz.	7	2½ oz.	7 oz.
24	750	1 lb. 13 oz.	7½ oz.	16 oz.	7–8	2½ oz.	7½ oz.
26	800	1 lb. 14 oz.	8 oz.	17 oz.	8	2½ oz.	8 oz.
28	850	2 lbs.	8½ oz.	18 oz.	8–9	3½ oz.	8½ oz.

Of course one can't feed all meat and expect his dogs to remain in condition, and obviously one can't feed an all-fat diet: the table shows the relative values of foods. "Dog biscuits" include crushed biscuits (kibbles). It is clear that the best buy is fat, but we shall discuss this matter later in this chapter.

Minerals. Everyone has heard and read of the importance of the various minerals to us and to our dogs. If one is feeding a good prepared ration, this aspect of diet can be forgotten; if one is feeding his Cockers what he eats himself, it can also be forgotten if the owner himself is healthy. But if one is feeding one's Cocker only what the dog likes most, the question of minerals becomes exceedingly important. If one is feeding that old mixture of kibbles, meat, cod-liver oil, and vegetables, again minerals must also be added.

TABLE 2

Cost of maintaining a 25 pound Cocker per day and for one year on the following feeding methods. (900 calories a day).

	Method	*Cost per day*	*Cost per year*
1.	Table Scraps	$.50	$182.5
2.	Canned dog food		
	(2 for 29¢)	.29	105.85
3.	Kibbles, Meat, Vegetables		
	(18¢, 50¢ & 5¢ per lb.)		
	Supplements (5¢ per day)	.38	138.70
4.	Pellets		
	(15¢ per lb.)	.084	30.66
5.	Dry Egg	.078	28.47
6.	Dry Dog Food plus Fat		
	(14¢ per lb.; fat, free)	.04 x 3	15.70

Table 3 shows the minerals and their principal sources and abundance in foods usually fed dogs. This is for those who want to mix their own foods. By *mixing* I mean putting together various foods such as milk, eggs, meat, vegetables, vitamin concentrates, mineral mixtures, and so forth. *Mixing* can also be taken to mean mixing dry food. *Vitamins.* If you use a good dry food, you can also just forget all about the word vitamins. These dietary essentials are so cheap that no food manufacturer who cares about his reputation leaves any out of his food mixtures. But if you mix your own rations, it may pay you to add a drop—no more—of percomorph oil for each dog daily, to provide vitamins A and D, and a spoonful of brewers' yeast for the B-complex vitamins. Your meats will supply B_1 and B_2. If you want to be sure your Cockers have enough of the essential fatty acids linoleic, linolenic, and arachidonic, give each dog two drops of raw linseed oil a day.

Table 4 lists the principal vitamins, their sources, and the amounts Cockers require daily.

TABLE 3

MINERALS: THEIR FUNCTIONS AND SOURCES

	FUNCTIONS IN BODY	PRINCIPLE SOURCES
Calcium		
90% of body calcium is in the bones; 1% in circulation Stored in body	Bone building. Rickets preventive Blood component Reproduction Lactation Muscle function Nerve function Heart function Tooth component	Bones and bone meal Alfalfa-leaf meal Milk
Phosphorus		
Bones, blood, muscles, and teeth	Bone building Tooth component Carbohydrate metabolism Fat metabolism Blood component Rickets preventive Liquid content of tissues	Cereals Meat Fish Bones Milk So abundant in dog diets it is of little concern to owners
Iron		
Composes only 4/1000ths of the body weight Needed in minute quantities Is stored in body	Component of red blood cells Transports oxygen in blood 65% is found in blood 30% is found in liver, bone marrow, and spleen 5% is found in muscle tissue	Egg yolk Liver Kidney Gizzard Heart Bone marrow Meats

	FUNCTIONS IN BODY	PRINCIPLE SOURCES
Potassium	Body-fluid regulator Helps regulate blood Muscular function	Blood Potatoes Vegetables
Sodium Found in body in combination with phosphorus, chlorine, and sulphur	Regulates body fluids Blood regulator Component of gastric juice Component of urine	Table salt Blood
Chlorine Found combined with sodium and hydrogen	Component of gastric juice Blood regulator Regulates body fluids Component of urine	Table salt Blood
Iodine Most of iodine in body is found in thyroid gland	Thyroid health and normal growth Regulates metabolism Prevents goiter and cretinism In formation of thyroxine	Foods grown in iodine-rich soils Iodized salt Fish meal made from salt-water fish Shellfish
Magnesium Needed only in minute amounts	Muscle activity Bone building Normal growth Nerve function Blood function	Bones Vegetables Epsom salts
Copper Needed only in minute amounts	Forms hemoglobin with iron	Blood Copper sulfate
Sulphur Minute amounts required but needed regularly	Body regulation Combination in salts as sulfates	Meat Egg yolk Any food which, when decomposed, smells like bad eggs

Table 4

VITAMINS: THEIR PROPERTIES, FUNCTIONS, AND SOURCES

VITAMINS	CONCERNED WITH	COMMON SOURCES
A (and carotene)		
Stable at boiling temperatures Spoils with age if exposed to air Body stores it Fat soluble	General living Growth Skin health Muscle co-ordination Fertility Digestion Hearing Vision Prevention of infection Nerve health Pituitary-gland function	Alfalfa-leaf meal Butter Carrots Egg yolks Fish livers Glandular organs Leaves of plants Milk, whole Spinach Many dark green vegetables Fish-Liver oils Synthetic vitamin A Carotine
B Complex		
Biotin Pantothenic acid Riboflavin, thiamin Folic acid Niacin Pyridoxin Animal protein factor Water soluble Body storage—small Some destroyed by high cooking temperatures, but not riboflavin Biotin effects robbed by raw egg white	Growth promotion Nerve health Heart health Liver function Appetite Gastro-intestinal function Intestinal absorption Lactation Fertility Muscle function Prevention of anemia Prevention of black tongue Prevention of Vincent's disease Kidney and bladder function Blood health	Yeast Cereals Milk Eggs Liver Alfalfa-leaf meal Rapidly growing plants Bacterial growth Cattle paunch and intestinal contents
D		
Irradiated ergosterol Well stored by body Stands considerable heat Resists decomposition Fat soluble	Regulation of calcium and phosphorus in blood Calcium and phosphorus metabolism Prevention of rickets Normal skeletal development Muscular co-ordination Lactation	Fish livers and oils extracted Some animal fats

VITAMINS	CONCERNED WITH	COMMON SOURCES
E		
Tocopherol Fat soluble Body stores it Perishes when exposed to air Stands ordinary cooking temperatures	Survival of young puppies	Seed germs Germ oils
K		
Fat soluble	Blood-clotting Young puppy health	Alfalfa-leaf meal
Unsaturated Fatty Acids (sometimes called vitamin F)		
Linoleic acid Linolenic acid Arachadinic acid	Coat and skin health	Wheat-germ oil Linseed oil Rapeseed oil Many seed oils

COMMON FEEDING METHODS

Table 2 shows graphically about how much it costs, per day and per year, to maintain a mature 25-pound Cocker. And it costs just about one and a third times as much to raise a puppy by these methods from weaning to eight months as it does to maintain a mature dog. The six pound puppy consumes as much as a 15 pound mature dog but the 24 pound pup eats as much as a 60 pound mature dog and then at maturity, his appetite suddenly dwindles.

Now we shall discuss these methods:

1. *Table scraps.* In this day of refrigeration, in almost every home there is no such thing as table scraps, unless the housewife is wasteful. All food for human beings can be kept until it is eaten. If it is spoiled for human consumption it should not be fed to dogs. Garbage today should be only bones, fruit peelings, and the like. Once any housewife starts feeding table scraps to a Cocker, she starts buying extra food, without even admitting to herself that some is for the dog. It then costs one fourth as much to feed a mature Cocker as it does to feed a member of the family; and this is an absurd extravagance. Practically the only real table scrap to save for the dog is the surplus grease you would otherwise throw away. And this, if wisely used, makes your dog cost less to feed, not more.

If you insist on feeding table scraps you might as well go all out for it and treat the dog as another member of the family If you neglect to make the family order big enough so the dog has something, then give him canned dog food to fill in and a few dog biscuits.

There are lots of old wives' tales about what not to feed a dog. No starch (therefore no potato), no fat, no sugar, or he'll get worms, no milk or he'll get more worms. All nonsense! A dog can digest any of these things as well as we can. If you feed him milk or candy, it is true that he gets finicky and won't eat his regular meal as he should. If he gets potatoes in lumps, he generally passes them as lumps in his evacuations, because dogs seldom chew easily swallowed food. So if you feed potatoes, mash them first.

How can sweets or milk "make worms"? I often ask clients, who tell me that they do, whether they ever eat sweets or drink milk. The way dogs get worms is from ingesting worm eggs, by swallowing fleas, or by eating infected rabbits from which they contract the tapeworms. It's to be hoped no worm eggs get into our milk containers or on our candy.

2. *Canned Dog Food.* This is food for those who don't care how much it costs to feed their Cockers. Look on the labels, and you will see that almost all canned foods contain from 70 per cent to 74 per cent water. So about a quarter of the can is food; the rest you can get free from your faucet. Now if four ounces of food is worth 17 cents to you—which makes it 68 cents a pound, the price of excellent meat—buy it. There are many fine foods in cans on the market, but don't let any manufacturer convince you that your Cocker can live on half a can a day, as some labels state. If fed canned food exclusively, any lively 25-pound Cocker needs two cans a day, and will eat more.

There are also some pretty awful canned foods, too. These are the ones you seldom see advertised. One company uses half-a-dozen different labels for the same food. If you happen to be a person who judges a food's value by how greedily your dog eats it, and if you are inclined to overfeed, then you may try one label and because the dog isn't hungry enough to eat the food, he refuses it and you say it's no good. By afternoon his appetite has improved. You try the same food with a different label and he eats it. "Wonderful food! That's the food for my dog from now on." Don't be deceived.

There are some good ones, too, which are not advertised but are sold cheaply, the makers hoping the low price will move the food. All companies that make good foods have experimental kennels, and are certain the diet is right before it is offered to the public.

3. *Kibbles, Meat, and Vegetables.* And of course cod-liver oil. Thousands of dogs have been raised and maintained on this mix-

ture, usually with liberal amounts of other vitamin and mineral concentrates added. Some kibbled biscuits are vastly better than others. On some the animals on test die in a few months. Some-

My Own Brucie—a nead study.

day kibbles may be made a complete diet. They have great taste appeal. The starch—flour being the chief ingredient—having been converted largely to dextrin by baking tastes sweet and the dogs generally find it to their liking. Add ground or canned meat and boiled green vegetables and you have a fairly good food.

This diet is troublesome to mix, it is a nuisance to buy and refrigerate meat or to open cans, and obtaining and cooking vegetables are laborious. And when you have added the tonics, have you done any better for your dogs than you would have done by feeding them some other way? Let's see.

4. *Pellets.* A number of commercial foods are now available in pellet form. Some are large pellets, an inch long and of various diameters. Some are only an eighth of an inch thick and not much longer. These may go by the name of *meal,* which is claimed to be homogenized. It is not, but the pelleting keeps the meal from sifting into layers, and it looks attractive to the housewife and pours easily. The makers suggest either dry feeding or else the addition of only a small amount of water, the dogs having to drink the balance to supply enough for digestion of the food. The pellets may be left in one pan and water in another, but in the case of small pellets the water pan soon becomes offensively dirty, and must be changed quite frequently.

5. *Meal Type.* This is often referred to in the trade as dry dog food. Since pellets are made from the same general formula, it might seem sensible to consider them with the meal types, but I do not because the latter are so much more versatile. Pellets have not found acceptance in kennel practice, while meals have. There are considerable differences among the many meals now on the market. Some have 30 per cent more protein than others, and some double the amount of fat which others carry. The minerals are sometimes so high as to be above the maximum for certain state laws. One of the most popular foods was thus outlawed from one of our states because it had 11 per cent calcium and phosphorus. And I knew dog owners feeding it who were adding tri-calcium phosphate as well! Ground bone is

the cheapest ingredient added to dog foods, so one need never add any more of the chemicals of which bone is composed—calcium and phosphorus.

Today almost all of the meals available have been industriously studied by nutritional scientists, and have been constantly

improved. If there is any one kind of food which tends to be better than the others, it is meal. Moreover, one can add fat to it and make an economical ration.

Taken at Jordan Marsh Co., first Television
Photos taken of Dogs March 1940
Idahurst Roderic 849986 – Idahurst Outcome 982338

If it costs you more than five cents a day to feed a pet Cocker, or four cents to feed kennel dogs, every cent you spend above that is wasted.

Mix 1½ ounces of fat with 5 ounces of a high-quality meal,

and you have 850 calories of the best food you can find. You couldn't beat it if you spent $100 a day.

This mixture will contain every known dietary essential. If you add any supplements, you are not only throwing away your money, but upsetting a formula which probably cost thousands of dollars to compound and test. I raised more than 2,000 beautiful Cockers on this diet. It supports reproduction wonderfully well; it reduces whelping troubles; pups are not born with cleft palates and harelips nearly so often as they are from dams raised on other diets. Such defects were almost unheard of in my dogs.

This diet also supports growth. Your Cockers will be full grown in seven months. I've had them full grown in 27 weeks. But they will eat food worth about 10 cents a day as they near maturity, and then when they reach it the food consumption drops enough to be alarming, if you are unprepared for it.

Meals and fat will support lactation (milk production) quite well, but more protein will be necessary for extra-large litters. This can be added as dried skim milk, dried whale meat, coddled eggs if you can buy them cheaply from a hatchery and cook them, or beef or horse meat. No more than 25 per cent to 30 per cent of these ingredients will be needed for large litters if the dam is a good milker.

WEANING PUPPIES

Remember that your Cocker bitch produces light cream, so when you wean the pups you have raised, start them off on rich food. So often dog owners feed them Pablum or Seraphim and cow's milk. Some even add lime water and dextrose, as if the little pups were human infants. Make their formula rich in fat and protein—almost the exact opposite of human milk.

Mix some light cream with a regular puppy food such as Pampa, the only one I know of readily available. Then there

Cockers, being rugged, are excellent subjects for the study of nutrition. Here are two pens in which the need for sunlight is being tested while the animals are being fed vitamin D deficient food.

will be no trouble with the transition from dog milk to your formula.

REDUCING

Every Cocker owner learns how gluttonous his pet really is—a mark of great vitality. So overfeeding is always a temptation, and no other breed of dog with such a high percentage of overweight animals is known. When Cockers become overweight, due to ignorance, lack of will power on the part of the owner, or neighbors' misplaced generosity, it is hard to refuse the appeal in those melting eyes, but do it. Don't let your dog get fat. And urge neighbors also to resist the appeal.

To reduce any Cocker is a simple matter. Just remember that any animal stores surplus food, in the form of fat, for a rainy day. He can literally live on that fat for months, not days. To reduce him requires exactly the same treatment as we give ourselves when we are overweight: use the accumulated fat for food; don't eat so much; make it a long, rainy day. If a Cocker needs 900 calories a day, give him a cup of dog meal and the water it takes to moisten it, and absolutely nothing else but water *ad lib*. He will be eating 500 calories, and must consume 400 from the fat on his body. Each pound of fat burns up to 4,000 calories, so he should reduce by about one tenth of a pound a day. That is if some miscreant in your home isn't slipping him tidbits, to defeat your attempt to increase his longevity via weight reduction.

EXERCISE

Cockers can live to a ripe old age if kept at their proper weight with no more exercise than they get walking about an apartment, but no breed loves exercise more. Remember that Cockers were selected to be busy hunters. You can exercise your dog by long walks, by training him to hunt if you enjoy bird hunting, but the easiest method for you when you are tired by a hard day's work is to spend fifteen minutes throwing a ball for your canine friend to retrieve.

You'll have no trouble teaching the retrieving part. As soon as the dog knows that to drop the ball in your hand means that you will throw it again for him, you can start the exercising process. A mile has 1,760 yards. Suppose you throw the ball 50 yards. He runs and retrieves it, and has run 100 yards. Repeat that eighteen times and your dog has run a mile, while you have remained in one place.

If you want some profitable exercise and live near a golf course, wait until evening, when the golfers have all gone home. Take Ruffles out and throw a golf ball: he will retrieve it. Now make believe to throw it. He will watch the direction you indicate, which will, of course, be out in the rough where golfers lose balls. Ruffles will return with a golf ball in his mouth. A Cocker belonging to one of my friends retrieved 42 golf balls in one evening. If no one else near your golf course knows this trick, you had better take along a bag to hold the balls your pockets won't contain.

This will also harden Ruffles' muscles and help him reduce, but, unless his diet be restricted, his increased appetite will more than atone for the expenditure of energy.

Chapter 6

YOUR COCKER'S HEREDITY

You may be the owner of a single pet Cocker puppy and have not the slightest intention of ever being a breeder. Yet the time will come when you will say, "He's been such a wonderful dog. How I'd like to have one of his own pups to take his place when the dreaded day of our parting comes."

You may be alone, or a man and wife who have decided to take up serious dog breeding as a hobby. You knew the old-time Cocker, and want to be in the van of those who will return it to top popularity. Good: you couldn't have chosen a more fascinating hobby, nor a worthier, more captivating breed with which to work.

You may be an established breeder who wants to know what is inherited, and how it occurs. I hope you want to learn how to breed out the three undesirable characteristics which, as we have seen, militate against Cocker popularity, and how to breed in all the brains which those little craniums are capable of holding.

It was more than twenty years ago when I addressed the New England Cocker Breeders' annual meeting in the clubrooms at 332 Newbury Street, Boston, Massachusetts. Since then my book *How to Breed Dogs* has had three revisions. Recently I came across the notes I used for that talk, and, amazing as it is, there is but little new or different today from what we knew at that time.

THE GERM PLASM

To get down to basic principles, every dog is the product of the germ plasm which created him and his family. It is carried in the male's testicles and the female's ovaries. Biologically speaking, the only reason for the dog's existence, or our own, is the perpetuation of the germ plasm. So much about the natural dogs, and about mankind, is a trick of nature to insure that perpetuation.

Under human direction and management the Cocker has become somewhat unnatural, but so have all domestic animals. Man chooses the products of certain germ plasm which best suit his fancy, and since in general these products (Cockers in this instance) carry the kind of germ plasm which is likely to produce more of the same kind, man produces what he wants by a process of constant selection.

The educated and experienced dog breeder thinks much more about the germ plasm than he does about the individual dogs. He combines this and that, hoping that someday there will be a combination that will produce the dog of his dreams—in this case the Cocker as nearly as possible like the ideal described by the standard.

This brings us to want to know what it is that makes the changes in different generations—what it is in the germ plasm that controls and creates all the characteristics of individuals.

The mechanism is chemical in nature. Microscopically tiny entities called *genes,* which are part of the cell nucleus, are the basic factors. At times of cell division (for any animal is a huge bundle of differentiated cells) the genes arrange themselves into pairs of chains which we call *chromosomes* (color bodies) because they take up certain stains which the rest of the cell does not. When the cell divides into two, one chromosome goes into each daughter cell, splits, and becomes two chromosomes.

But when the germ cells in the testicles divide to become sperm, only one chromosome of each pair is carried by a sperm. And when the *ova* (eggs) each get ready to unite with a sperm, the egg casts off half of its chromosomes, and, upon combining with the sperm, produces the architectural plans for a new individual. So this new individual inherits half from the germ plasm of each parent.

If you will just remember that *each characteristic of the dog is determined by not one, but two genes in the dog's germ plasm,* it will make it much easier for you to understand this otherwise complicated matter.

Geneticists, the students of heredity, have found that sometimes one gene will be different from its partner in its influence on the production of a given characteristic of the individual. Easiest to explain is coat color, but the principle is the same for many other traits. A dog may have one gene which produces a black coat, and another which produces a mixture of black and white (particolor, in Cockers). When the pair work together, the black is able to overpower the parti gene, so the pup this combination produces is black. Therefore such genes are called *dominant;* those overpowered are called *recessive.* If two partis are mated, only partis can result, but if two blacks are mated, each dog having a gene for parti, then some partis can result.

It is all a matter of chance. Here are a pair of genes represented by marbles. The black-producing gene is a black marble, the parti a white marble. Each goes into a separate sperm cell. The dog is mated to a black bitch with the same combination. The chances are the same in her case, so let's represent her genes also by a black and a white marble.

Mix the four marbles in a bowl. Now reach in and take out pairs of marbles. What will you have? You might draw out two blacks, two whites, or a black and a white. The mathematical chances are that from a hundred such tries you would have two blacks 25 times, a black and a white 50 times, and two whites 25 times.

Suppose you mate a black dog, which carries white recessively, with a parti bitch, what then? Figure it out: you'll have 50 per cent pure partis and 50 per cent blacks carrying the parti gene recessively, and these of course will be blacks.

So there are six ways, and only six, in which such dogs can be mated:

1. Two pure blacks, which will produce only pure blacks.
2. Two blacks, each of which carries parti genes (hybrid). The expectancy will be 25 per cent pure black, 50 per cent hybrid, and 25 per cent pure parti.
3. A hybrid black and a pure parti will produce 50 per cent hybrid black and 50 per cent partis.
4. A hybrid black and a pure black will produce 50 per cent hybrids and 50 per cent purebreds.

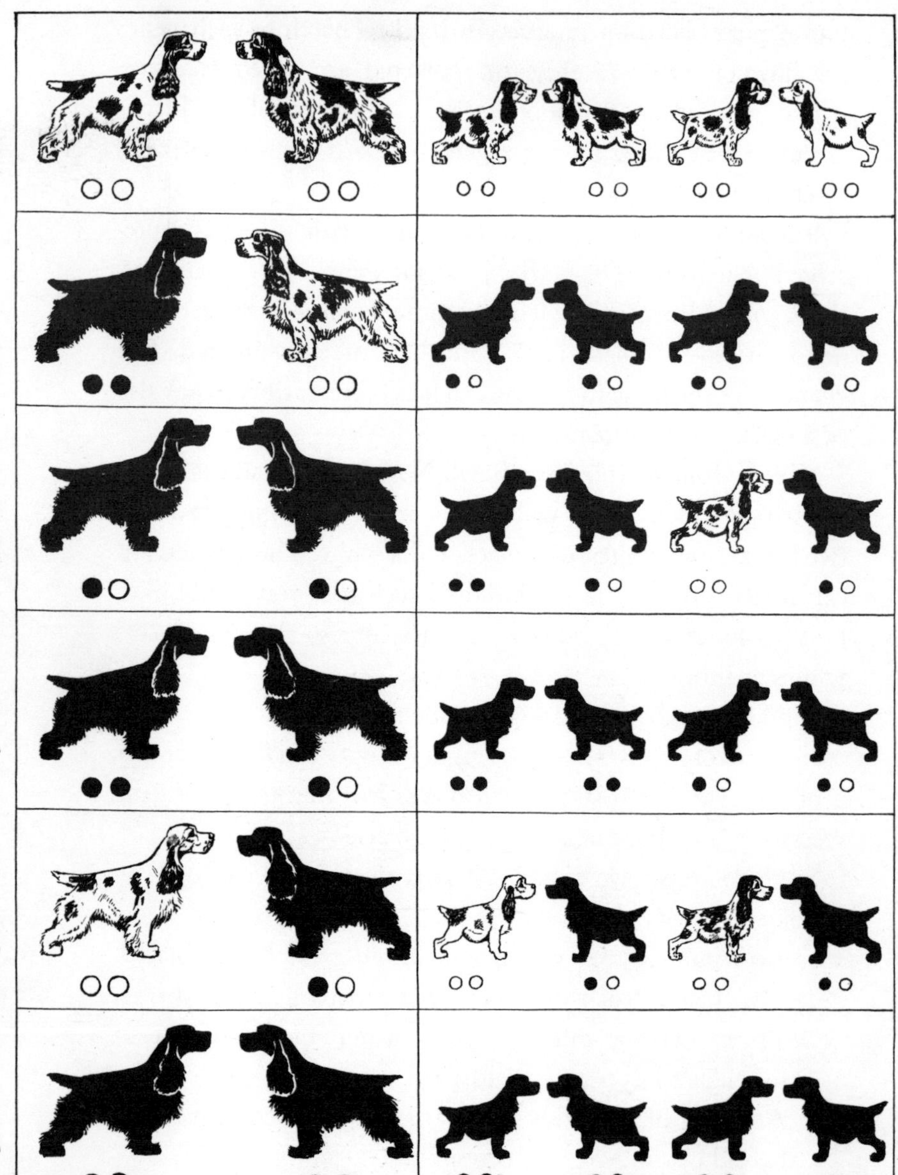
PARENTS
OFFSPRING
1
2
3
4
5
6

5. A pure black and a pure parti will produce only hybrids.
6. Two pure partis will produce only partis.

In any one mating these mathematical expectancies may not be realized, but among a hundred matings they would be close. I have mated two blacks and had a litter of four partis and one black when I expected the reverse, but that does not invalidate the principle, for in the long run my calculations worked out as they should have done.

This principle of dominance and recessiveness in the pairs of genes which determine traits has been studied by many students of canine genetics, as it applies to a great many characteristics, not only those of coat color, but of eye color and certain behavior patterns as well. What has been found to apply to other breeds applies equally to Cockers.

Below is a list of dominants and recessives from which, provided you know the genetic make-up of your dogs, you can get a good idea of what they will produce.

Dominance and Recessiveness of Certain Cocker Characters

Black is dominant over all other Cocker colors.
Normal dominant over inhibiting factor which produces liver color.
Non-dilution dominant over dilution factor.
Solid dominant over particolor.
Bicolor dominant over tricolor.
Solid dominant over black-and-tan.
Ticking dominant over lack of ticking.
Black eyed white recessive to colored.
Albinism recessive to colored.

Dewclaws on hind legs dominant over lack of dewclaws.
Umbilical hernia recessive to normal.

Trail barking dominant over mute trailing.

Besides these characters there are some whose mode of inheritance is known only in a general way:

Water-going propensity dominant over non-water going.
Tendency to urinate when excited recessive to normal.
Gun-shyness tends to be recessive.
Shorter coat dominant over longer by degrees.
Curly coat dominant over straight.
Tendency to have warts runs in families.

Then there are others which are determined by a great many genes. Here is a dog with perfect gait. Is this dominant over a hitching type of gait? Probably such characteristics are determined by a multiplicity of genes. And the same applies to hunting ability. A poor hunter mated to a good one may produce mediocre workers; the result can't be said to be a genetic certainty. Half a million dollars was spent studying racing ability in horses, but the results simply showed that it pays to mate the best with the best, and that racing ability runs in families; there is no dominance and recessiveness to it, because racing ability represents the development of so many genes that prediction is impossible.

OLD IDEAS

In the old days everybody believed that inheritance came about through blood. Many people who ought to know better still speak of pure-blooded dogs, as if blood had something to do with inheritance. A red blood cell is no larger than a dog sperm. Blood gives one a mind picture of dilution, instead of the correct one of presence or absence. Inheritance in dogs is not a matter of mixing of bloods, which would produce blends. We would be better off without such an idea.

Our grandparents thought that a fright experienced by a pregnant bitch would mark her pups; that the effects of one litter carried over to the next; that some of the previous stud's blood stayed around to mix with that of the next stud and ruin the pups. They often killed bitches which had been mismated, because they thought such bitches were ruined for future breeding.

Yes, and they thought acquired characteristics were inherited. Hunt Cockers hard and their pups would be better hunters. Practice dogs in standing for shows, and their pups would stand better at shows. Snip off dogs' coats regularly, and their pups would tend to have shorter hair.

These "aids" to breeding are no longer held in respect by geneticists, and certainly the Cocker clippers know that their dogs' coats are getting longer the more generations are clipped. But this is due to selection, and not to clipping at all. This fact alone should disabuse the mind of anyone who entertains any of these old wives' tales.

MUTATIONS

If not by the inheritance of acquired characteristics, how then did all of these amazing differences among dogs come about? How did the very long bushy Cocker coat come into existence? How did the increased station (leg length) develop? Where did the various colors come from? They were mutations.

Mutations are sudden changes. Some occur in the germ plasm and breed true. Some are dominant and some recessive. They are exceedingly rare but they do occur and the dog's owner recognizes one and by selective breeding incorporates it as a characteristic.

I have had several mutations which bred true occur in my own dogs. One had a tight screw tail. Leg Length in Cockers is inherited as it is in breed crosses, the shorter legs being dominant over the longer. But imagine my amazement to find and extra short legged Cocker (see illustration) among a litter of pups and then to learn by breeding it, that the characteristic was recessive.

There was no determiner in the germ plasm of the original Cocker stock which could produce the ultra long hair some show winners exhibit. It came by steps, each step being a mutation which was incorporated in a strain by breeding.

Most mutations are downward in the evolutionary scale; only rarely is one an improvement. Many Cocker breeders consider the long hair an expression of degeneration just as the short legs on the Cockers shown in the illustration are.

INBREEDING (Mating between cousins or closer relatives.)

Over and over again Cocker owners say to me, in excusing the nasty dispositions of their dogs, "Too much inbreeding," or "They're inbreeding these dogs too much these days; spoils their dispositions." Obviously some of these evil-tempered dogs are badly trained. Actually inbreeding has very little, if anything, to do with the explanation.

A normal and a short legged Cocker from the same litter. This mutation occurred in one of the author's dogs and proved to be a recessive.

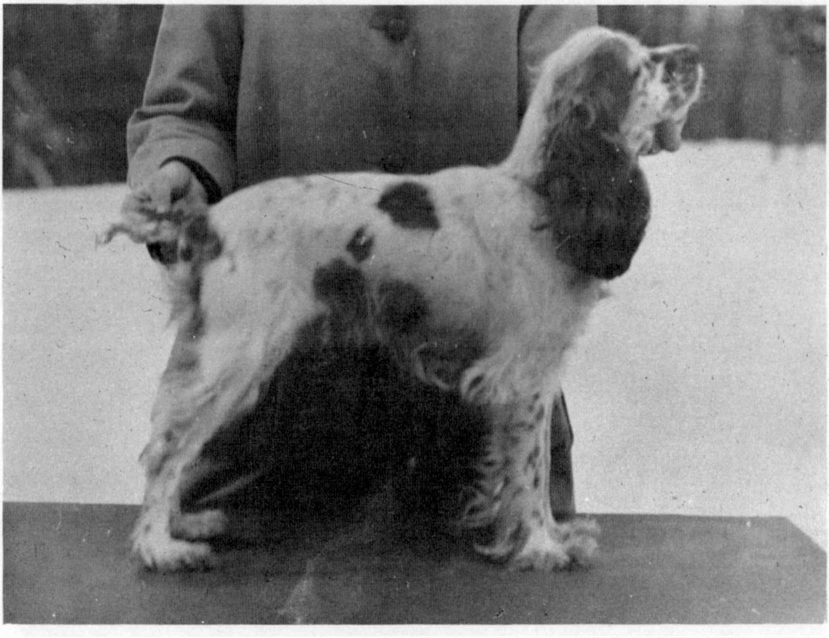

All that inbreeding does is to double up the genes in the germ plasm. If there are desirable genes, it enhances the chances of producing desirable traits; if there are undesirable ones, these, too, come out. Usually it wasn't inbreeding which produced so many nasty Cockers: it was careless, sloppy breeding.

A recessive short legged pup which appeared in third generation. Her double grandfather was the black-and-white short legged pup shown above.

The money breeders don't care what the pups are temperamentally, as long as they *look* as they are supposed to. What does a pet-shop owner usually know about the parents and grandparents of the pups in his window? What does the average puppy buyer demand, beyond the fact that the puppy be cute and cuddly? For a fortnight's playing dolls with a pup, he frequently pays with twelve years' ownership of something which is only obnoxious to anyone who knows dogs. No wonder so many people are "fed up" with Cockers. It is going to take several years to show the public that they bought animals that only looked somewhat like Cockers; they didn't buy typical specimens.

Judicious inbreeding does not weaken dogs: it fixes traits so they breed true. It makes greater uniformity in a strain. But it does reduce vigor to some extent. Yet after long enough inbreeding—after the undesirable and weakening influences have been eliminated, inbreeding having brought them to light—the animals are all so much alike that they are equivalent to identical twins. There are white rats and mice, used in laboratories, which have been mated brother to sister for more than a hundred generations, and no better laboratory animals can be found.

No one has yet announced the inbreeding of dogs, brother to sister, more than four generations. I tried it with Beagles and the litters became very small, screw tails appeared in several, and by the fourth generation the dogs were smaller than the originals. If one had enough money and enough dogs, Cockers could be bred in this fashion without harm to them, provided that one kept up a rigorous selection. But it is impractical for the ordinary breeder. I cite it to show that not inbreeding but careless breeding, breeding with no thought of selection, is the reason why we have too many unreliable Cockers.

LINE BREEDING is simply mating dogs reasonably closely related and keeping within a strain. All the great dog breeders combine line breeding and inbreeding. In fact, one must, to establish a strain. All of our modern Cockers were inbred and line bred, as you will find if you study pedigrees.

OUT BREEDING is mat ing dogs related only distantly, or, so far as pedigrees show, not at all.

TWINS

There are two kinds of twins in human beings, sheep and cattle; that is, in the species which ordinarily produce but one offspring at a time. Dogs produce litter mates and, rarely, identical twins as do the other species. Identical twins are enclosed in the same fetal membrane and are quite similar if not identical. Several pair have been born among my dogs and since I first reported a pair of Idahurst puppies in How To Breed Dogs, several persons have written me. Some have actually found two pups in one membrane and connected to the same placenta. Such puppies result from the splitting of the newly fertilized egg into two cells each of which develops into a puppy.

So much for some basic principles. Now let us in the next chapter take up the inheritance of some of the individual characteristics that interest all of us breeders.

Chapter 7

YOUR COCKER'S HEREDITY—CONTINUED

MENTAL APTITUDES

The simple list in the last chapter is interesting, but some amplification is necessary. Because behavior patterns are the most important aspect of any dog, we shall consider what is known about mental heredity first.

Some of the behavioristic school of philosophers tell us there is no such thing as inheritance of mental aptitudes or behavior patterns. But these persons never bother even to glance at what we know about dogs: they worked with human beings. But the day of such shallowness is going. One scientist's study of identical human twins upsets all of the claims of non-inheritance made by behaviorists. Yet even this study should not have been necessary to convince the partly-learned psychologists that behavior patterns are just as hereditary as eye color, if in a more complex manner.

My study of the inheritance of trail barking was the first to demonstrate that such behavior is hereditary and independent of training. I mated dogs of breeds which bay on the trail of game with dogs of breeds which trail mutely, and all of the pups bark on the trail. What follows has no interest to the owner of a pet Cocker, but considerable interest to a hunter:

Every one of the early Spaniels used in cocking "gave tongue" when it scented a bird. For this reason, color in a hunting Spaniel was less important than it is today. You can easily imagine the scene as the early Spaniel was used as an accessory in falconry, the dog busily quartering about in the bush until he scented a bird, then barking as he got closer. A pheasant would run, and the dog would follow him until the bird left the ground.

The hunters would know by the dog's voice that he had "made game" and would remove the falcon's hood. As the quarry shot into the air the incredibly swift falcon would race it and, pouncing down, either injure the bird or catch it in its talons.

If the bird were injured, the Spaniel would retrieve it. Some hunters used to teach their dogs to sit until commanded to retrieve, because if dog, game bird and falcon had met in a free-for-all some damage might well have been expected.

Cockers were no exception to trail barking. Indeed we are told that they were bred for a merry tone, and that the tone changed on different kinds of game. This is entirely credible. I can tell from the tone of several of my own hounds whether they have treed a squirrel, a porcupine, a skunk or a coon.

Stonehenge, in *On the Dog,* which was published in 1790, says, "A Spaniel possessing a musical but not noisy voice is all the more valuable if it distinguishes in its notes between the various kinds of game." The various kinds of game referred to probably included rabbits. A sight hound must not drop its head to find game but pursue only with its nose, so Spaniels were used to "spring" the rabbits which the Greyhounds, seeing, were "slipped" to chase.

But while most Springer Spaniels today open (give voice) on the trail, Cockers do not—on birds, at any rate. I have known them to trail up with Beagles and do a little yipping when they see a rabbit, but otherwise trail mutely. I have known other Cockers which ran on deer trails yipping merrily. Just when the change from open trailing to mute trailing occurred in Cockers we don't know. It must have happened through rigid selection, and Cockers were mostly still or mute trailers as early as 1900. In 1899 we find a comment on a field trail by the association's president, Mr. Arkwright: "All ran mute with the exception of one puppy."

A field trial or hunting Cocker who barks as he hunts, even in recognizing the bird, is practically disqualified. If this characteristic follows inheritance in all other breeds, and it appears to, the open-trailing behavior is dominant over the still trailing. So, once the trait is lost, we should not expect it to show up again from any matings of still trailers. If it is desired, the only way to introduce it is to find a Cocker that opens on a bird's scent and use him in the matings, inbreeding the progeny until they are pure bred for this individual characteristic.

But this does not mean that the dog will open on all kinds of game. A Cocker that opens on rabbits may not do so on birds. By years of selection I have developed my Bloodhounds until they never open on a man trail (training has nothing to do with it), but every one will be wide open on a coon or fox trail if he is encouraged to run it.

Other behavior patterns are clearly inherited, and some not

so clearly. I mentioned the reaction of puppies to a hypodermic needle. It is amazing to note how similar the reaction is from one generation to the next. The descendants of Idahurst Belle, of which I have had many, usually stood on the table and took the injection without even wincing. Some pups of other strains brought to the hospital for vaccination will turn their heads and snap at the doctor's hand. This variation in reaction occurs in all breeds of Spaniels, and indeed in all breeds of dogs. I recall a Springer breeder bringing a station-wagon load of 36 pups for vaccination. All were close to three months old, and in one crate there were five pups of a new breeding which he had recently acquired. All of his own pups stood like rocks when vaccinated, but the five of the strain new to him *all* squealed and urinated.

Among all of the bird-hunting breeds, the Spaniels are the only ones which are bred to keep their noses close to the ground, hound fashion, when they hunt. Setters and Pointers hunt with heads high. This is definitely a dominant trait. In crosses I made of Cockers with Setters, the puppies all hunted with heads up, like Setters. Even in crosses of Setters with Bloodhounds the progeny were useless as trailing dogs. When you see a Cocker hunt with head carried high, he probably has the genes of the English Setter in him.

The behavior pattern of interest in birds and flying objects, which Setters and Pointers generally show so strongly, is not well developed in the Cocker. I noticed that when a butterfly flew through pens containing both Setter and Cocker pups, the Setters would show intense interest, while the Cockers displayed only a little more interest than hounds of any breed. This indicates that less selection has been applied to the Cocker to make it interested in flying objects, and in this respect the breed is more houndlike, showing a greater degree of interest in ground and body scents.

Perhaps that is why the crosses of Cocker with Beagle make such excellent rabbit and squirrel dogs. I have known many that ran almost as well as field-trial Beagles, whereas crosses of Beagles and English Setters were worthless in rabbit trailing.

My Own Peter Manning was a cobby specimen of the approved type.

In New England, one of the principal uses of Cockers in hunting was in treeing. Even today, in the backwoods sections, bird hunters wouldn't hunt partridges any other way, unsporting as it is. Their Cockers are economic assets. In these areas the birds see so little of human beings that they are far less shy than those the average hunter knows.

The treeing method goes like this: the Cocker runs well ahead of the hunter, trailing about for bird scents. When he smells one, he runs toward it. The partridge (ruffled grouse) hears and sees this animated object scurrying about and flies up to the limb of a tree, perhaps eight or ten feet off the ground, and sits surveying the dog, who is soon looking up and barking at the bird. One of my backwoods friends with whom I hunted coons every year kept his family "in partridge" every fall until they were sick of it, and all with a black Cocker. I accompanied him many times on these hunts, in which he delighted. The bird would cock its head quizzically from side to side, often holding it below the limb on which it sat studying that strange creature, the dog.

And while its attention was glued on the dog, my friend, like hundreds of others who still hunt in this way, would walk close enough to the scene to pop the bird in the head with a .22 rifle bullet.

The point is that these Cockers are natural tree dogs, and many make squirrel dogs *par excellence,* a use to which only those with natural coats can be put, and to which not enough are put. They tree almost as well as tree hounds bred for the purpose, and this aptitude is not so well recognized as it should be, although it is by squirrel hunters. Crossed with American Fox Terriers, the short-haired pups make grand squirrel dogs, illustrating the inheritance of this aptitude.

While most persons never give the aptitude of posing very much thought, observant Cocker breeders tell you how much easier it is to get certain dogs to pose as show dogs should than others. There are many who will stand in a show pose when no hand is on or under them. This characteristic quite definitely runs in families.

And there are tremendous differences between the reactions of dogs to an electric clipper the first time one is used on them.

No matter how gently a person works, starting on the rear end, stroking the dog, talking gently, and taking several times the usual period to perform the task, there are some Cockers which are so terrified that they must be anesthetized, in the name of kindness, before the job can be completed. In our hospital we keep special note of the dogs that behave so. Next time we clip

My Own Lady Alice—beautifully proportioned and a worthy winner.

them, we may try again to see if they are still panic-stricken. If they are, we give Pentothal again, which the dog enjoys, and he awakens in his new state. Such dogs tend to have the same kind of pups.

Gun-shyness is akin to such temperaments, although occasionally an otherwise temperamentally sound dog may be afraid of loud noises. Gun-shy dogs are invariably thunder-shy. This defect exhibits itself early, and definitely runs in families. At loud reports the dogs really seem to suffer mentally. It is better not to use them for breeding. It is possible to help a gun-shy dog by early training, but such conditioning does not remove the basic defect, and germ plasm which transmits it had better not be perpetuated.

The tendencv to piddle is another definitely hereditary weakness which, unfortunately, is generally completely overlooked by breeders. There is scarcely a Cocker kennel today in which some of the dogs do not wet when approached by strangers, or even by their owners. But there are also thousands of Cockers that show no such incontinence. In a kennel of hunting dogs there is less need to be particular about this defect, but in house dogs it should be diligently watched for and eliminated by selective breeding. That it runs in families none can doubt; that it is a matter of simple inheritance is open to question. Probably this failing is concerned with multiple genes.

Fondness for retrieving shows up in all typical Cockers, yet there are strains so un-Cockerly that they show not the slightest natural interest in it and can be trained only with difficulty. This lack runs in families. To me it is amazing to see a Cocker whose ancestors have never seen any other birds than English sparrows in a city back yard, who have never had an opportunity to retrieve even one of those sparrows for many generations, yet when the pup is given the chance to do his natural work, he usually acts as if he came from a long line of well-trained hunters. So well does his inheritance persist in him. Still, there are some who, because of so many generations without selection, have lost the hunting ability—not from the inheritance of disuse, but because of inbreeding of inferior hunters.

So keen is the desire to retrieve in Cockers—to carry something gently in their mouths—that if nothing is accorded them to carry, they may even pick up stools. This sometimes leads to the filthy habit called coprophagy (dung eating). I have corrected it many times in my own Cockers, and helped clients with theirs, by the simple expedient of leaving a few old tennis balls in the runs. The natural retrievers will be found carrying such balls by the hour. Clients have told me that their Cockers annoyed them by stealing shoes, but they really weren't stealing them: what they were doing was simply trying to satisfy their desire to retrieve. That is why Cockers learn to "go get things," such as your shoes, on command. No other breed is more easily taught to fetch your bedroom slippers, bring in the paper, or take the mail from the postman. I have even seen a Cocker carry a pound of butter and leave only slight dents in the cardboard. Dogs of most breeds, given such an opportunity, are willing enough to carry the butter, but do so in their stomachs!

Another quite remarkable Cocker characteristic used to be manifested in the days when we had great epizootics (animal epidemics) of what was then called distemper. When dogs of many breeds have the first rise in temperature which that dreaded disease causes they show it by having fits—convulsions. Beagles almost all had them, yet Cockers, with exactly the same infection, would not. The subsequent mortality was about equal, but the first symptoms are different in Cockers—a fact difficult to explain.

The propensity to swim is also hereditary, but is not so marked in Cockers as in specialized water-dog retrievers or even Springer Spaniels. There is great variation among Cockers in this regard, and the water-going aptitude is pronounced in a minority. This is one of the reasons why Cockers make so much better house dogs than other retrievers for families who live near bodies of water or even muddy brooks. I know of no study within the Cocker breed, but when dogs of water-going breeds, like Newfoundlands, are crossed with those of non-water-going breeds, the pups are water dogs—showing the dominance of the characteristic. And quite possibly the inheritance is the same in Cockers.

So much for the more important aspects of Cocker heredity. What do we know about the physical traits? Here are some, the mode of inheritance of which has been studied.

COAT CHARACTERISTICS

In the pure-bred Cocker and in breed crosses we find that the *thickness of the coat*—the number of hairs per inch—tends to be inherited, with the thinner coat being dominant. Dogs such as Norwegian Elkhounds, whose coats are extremely dense, when mated to hounds with sparse hair produce houndlike coats. When two of these are mated, about 25 per cent of the pups appear with the dense coats.

In Cockers this holds quite definitely. The woolly-coated dogs often come from parents with proper Cocker coats. This is why it is so easy to breed Woolly Cockers; a pair seldom produces sparse-coated pups.

Wavy hair was dominant over straight hair in all of the matings I have made. I had one dog, pure for the trait, with a particularly wavy red coat, and many bitches were bred to him because people, especially women, thought it was so beautiful. I never knew him to sire a straight-coated dog. The reason Cockers have waves in the coat is simply that the guard hair is oval shaped instead of round. This is also the reason why human hair curls.

I have had several wavy-haired Cocker matings produce straight-haired dogs.

Length of coat is also inherited, the shorter being dominant, but in all such cases one must realize that color has an effect on hair length. White probably inhibts it; so does red. As I mentioned before, black hair growing in white coats may be many times as long as the white. So the same dog, if it were black, would have a much longer coat. I remember when Cocker breeders used to wonder how they could breed red dogs with longer coats. One of the facts I learned many years ago was that blacks which came from a red with long hair had such long coats that they almost dragged the ground. Mate two such deformities and the pups have identical coats, because two recessives do not produce dominants.

The only explanations for the modern barbered Cockers are that (1) they are the product of mutations, since there were no such coats on the foundation dogs in the breed, or (2) there were poodles crossed into the breed to obtain the long, woolly coat.

This, then, is not a simple matter of inheritance. Coat length seems to be inherited, with the shorter coat in each degree being dominant over the longer. If an American Fox Terrier were mated with the Cocker with the longest, most woolly coat, the pups would have short, smooth coats. If a pure, medium-length-coated Cocker were mated to the extreme type, the pups would have medium-length coats. This obtains if the dogs are all of the same color.

Coarseness of Coat. Here again we find the coarser dominant over the finer. It occurs when different breeds are crossed within the breed of Cockers, and this again explains why it is so easy to breed fine-textured woolly coats.

Stockdale Stormalong

My Own Brucie
(Wide World)

Dream Boy of Chalburn
(Wide World)

Pinefair Prophet
(Wide World)

COAT COLOR

Black. Black is dominant over all other Cocker colors. A black mated to a white may produce pups with slightly more white on the chest than when two blacks are mated.

Solid color, whether black, red, liver or black and tan is dominant over white spotting.

Solid Color is dominant over white spotting. Black-and-white pups will have larger pigmented areas than will equivalent red-and-white pups. The illustration shows this clearly.

Ticking modifies the white so it appears roaned. Such dogs are called blue ticked or orange ticked. Ticking is dominant over its lack. So two whites do not produce ticked pups, but ticked sometimes produce about 25 per cent unticked. It is not possible to tell whether a solid-colored dog carries the ticking factor; he may, and it will be masked, or, if there is a white spot on the chest, this may be roaned.

Liver is a black with the pigment inhibited. It behaves like black in inheritance except where two blacks are mated. Livers

always have pale noses, foot pads, and light eyes. It is impossible to breed them with dark eyes, so they must be judged as light-eyed without penalization.

Black-and-tan. Since two reds sometimes produce dogs of this color, it is obvious that the saddle factor which sometimes makes the dog almost all black is a modifier of red. Black-and-tans can come from two blacks if they carry red recessively, or from a black and a red, but there is no need for one of the parents to be black.

Couple this color with the white spotting factor, and we have a tricolor—among the most beautiful of all Cockers.

Cream is a dilute red produced by a dilution gene (factor) and is recessive to red, the non-dilution factor.

Blue is a color seldom seen. It is a dilute black. If the same genes that dilute red to make cream become combined with black, they will produce blue Cockers.

Liver-and-tan is like black-and-tan in inheritance. The face and spots over the eyes are usually tan, as are the legs and an arc under the tail.

All-white. A few white Cockers with black noses and foot pads and dark eyes and eyelids have been bred, but most of the almost-whites lack pigmentation of the eyelids, causing unattractive expressions. Simcoe Purity, of which almost every Cocker breeder has heard, was not this kind of dog. He was a dark-eyed white. Another was produced by mating him to his half-sister.

Only one albino Cocker, with his pink eyes, has been reported to me—which is rather strange, since I have records of many albino Pekinese.

Both of these whites are recessive to all other colors. If a dark-eyed white in any other species is mated with an albino, the offspring are dark-colored. It would probably be so in Cockers.

DEWCLAWS

In the case of front-feet dewclaws—the extra digits, equivalent to human thumbs, being too high on the foot to be of any use—there is little reason for their removal, but because those on the hind feet give so much trouble they are generally removed at the time puppies' tails are docked. If left, the toenail often grows in a circle, penetrating the skin and causing annoyance and pain to the dog.

Hind-feet dewclaws are inherited in dominant fashion, two dogs without them never producing pups with them. But, con-

Puppy with umbilical hernia.

versely, dogs having dewclaws often produce pups without. Occasionally a Cocker is born with only one of these appendages, but it such a dog is mated the pups usually have them on both hind legs. The fact that a dog has none is no indication of whether he can pass dewclaws to his pups; his may have been removed when a pup. It requires a careful examination to make the determination.

HERNIAS

A high percentage of Cockers are born with small umbilical hernias, just as are thousands of puppies of other breeds. Because of the long hair of Cockers which covers the hernias such defects are usually overlooked. They seldom cause any inconveniencee. One study showed the defect to be inherited as a recessive on a simple Mendelian basis. That it is inherited can scarcely be doubted; that dogs carrying the recessive defect should not be bred is another matter. So many Cockers do carry it or are herniated themselves that probably half the Cocker population would have to be rejected if such a policy were carried out.

Moreover there is some doubt that the defect is always a recessive. Among one strain of Beagles which I have followed, two herniated dogs produced four out of seven pups without hernias. More investigational work remains to be done on this subject.

Chapter 8

REPRODUCTION IN THE COCKER BITCH

In order to be a fairly successful breeder it is not essential that you understand the processes of reproduction. You can proceed by hit-or-miss, by reliance upon tradition, which stems from a conglomeration of old wives' tales and general attempts to explain phenomena without the underlying knowledge we have today. Or you can leave it all to your veterinarian; but that will be unnecessarily expensive.

One of the most attractive features of dog breeding is the fact that those who get the most out of it are those who travel down the bypaths into which it leads them in search of knowledge. There are so many of these temptations, and they are all intriguing. Reproduction is one of the most rewarding and fascinating of them. Many people who know very little about human reproduction have considerable information about canine, and of course they catch the implications. Many parents find that letting their children learn about reproduction from watching the phenomenon in dogs, and helping with a few bits of information as the children acquire knowledge, is one of the finest ways of dealing with the matter. Our children learned in that way. We explained, when they asked, about the inside happenings—ovulation, gestation, and so forth—and they never did ask the silly questions so often put by children who acquire their information on street corners, or behind the barn, from other children.

Despite today's broad education, the public know practically nothing about their own reproduction, and what they think they know is mostly erroneous, so how can they be expected to understand it in dogs? I often ask women clients, to whom I am about to explain the "facts of life" about their bitches, if they know what day of the cycle the human female ovulates. Surely 95 per cent of them never heard the word, judging by their expressions of bewilderment.

Probably this is all "old hat" to you; if so, skip it. If not, read it, because if you are a serious dog breeder it may save you time and money.

The female Cocker's ovaries—that part of her for which all the rest of her exists—are located inside her abdomen, high up and just behind her last ribs. They are about as large as a yellow-eye bean but a little more compressed (flatter). Each ovary is encircled by a capsule, in one side of which there is a slit, with spongy tissue along its edge, called fimbria. Starting from this tissue, a tiny tube runs in a zigzag course over each capsule and terminates at the upper end of one of the branches of the uterus (womb). These tubes are called Fallopian. The uterus is constructed in the shape of a letter Y. The illustration shows the difference in anatomical construction between the human and

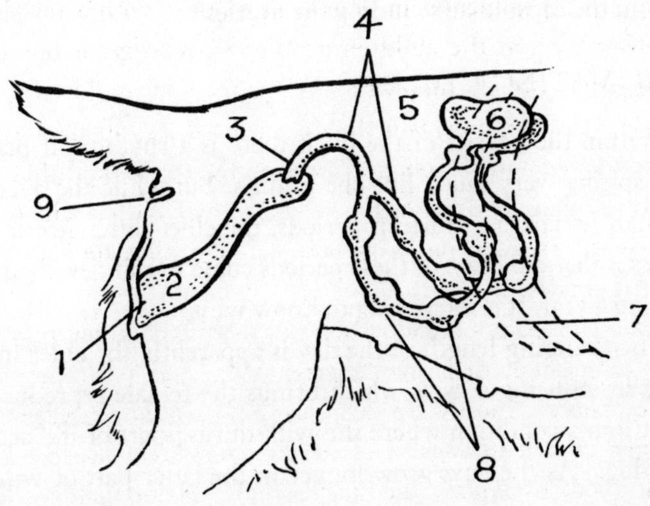

Female organs of reproduction. Reproductive system of a bitch. (1) Vulva. (2) Vagina. (3) Cervix. (4) Uterus. (5) Ovary. (6) Kidney. (7) Location of ribs. (8) Lump consisting of embryo and placenta. (9) Anus.

canine female reproductive tracts. It is considerable. Many of those persons who have some knowledge of the human tract think the long arms of the uterus in the bitch are Fallopian tubes, but such is not the case.

When a bitch becomes pregnant, the fertilized eggs nest at various places along the uterus, which expands to accommodate their growth and to protect them as well. A Cocker with a dozen pups in her uterus will have developed each of its horns to perhaps thirty inches long and two inches in diameter.

When *copulation* (the mating of dog with bitch) occurs, sperm are transferred and are moved up the uterus by the same sort of movement (peristalsis) that occurs in the intestines. Within a few minutes after tieing (sexual fusion) occurs, the sperm are already up the uterus, through the Fallopian tubes, and in the capsule surrounding the ovaries.

THE MATING CYCLE

Within the ovaries of the bitch there is a rhythmical period transpiring, very much like the human. But while the average human female has thirteen periods, the chief difference in canines is that only two of these periods come to full development during a year. It is interesting to know why.

The changing length of the day is apparently the chief influence in inducing a cycle which brings the female reproductive tract into a condition where she will, during part of it, "accept the dog." As the days grow longer in the latter part of winter, and when they get noticeably shorter in late summer, the vast majority of bitches come into heat.

This fact can be used to bring a bitch into heat. If the length of her day is increased by artificial light, one hour a day for the first week, two hours the second, three the third, and four the fourth, she will usually be in heat. Or shipping a bitch from, say, the vicinity of Boston to some city in Georgia will usually accomplish the same result in less than six weeks. The reverse is true: sending a bitch from the South to the North sometimes produces the same effect, especially when it is done during the winter, when days are short, and provided the bitch is not kept in a lighted kennel or in your home.

The germ plasm, stored in the ovaries, ripens eggs which develop in blisterlike pockets that grow toward the surface of the ovaries. Of these there are a great many more than there are eggs which become puppies. At a certain time, about the fourteenth to sixteenth day (much as is the case with the human female), these pockets, called follicles, are as large as small peas, and protrude from the bean-shaped ovary. The follicles produce *follicular hormone,* which acts to prepare the uterus. When they cannot stand the internal pressure any longer, due to the thinning of their walls, most of the follicles

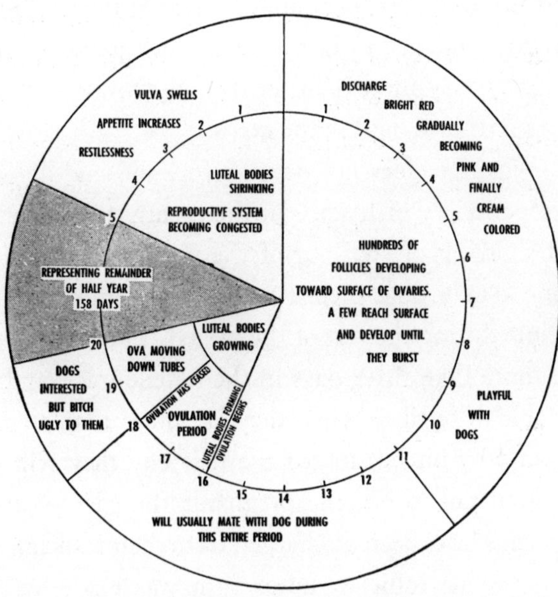

The mating cycle in the average bitch. Smaller breeds tend to ovulate earlier than large. Ovulation in the Cocker probably begins on the fourteenth day rather than the sixteenth as shown here. Some bitches ovulate even later than the sixteenth.

which have protruded from the ovary burst and liberate the eggs (ova) into the capsule around it.

They are beset by a multitude of male sperm, provided, of course, the bitch has just been bred. It was formerly thought that one sperm was sufficient to penetrate an egg, but we now know that a large number of sperm are required to break down the egg's resistance, because the sperm have an enzyme which weakens the egg's coating, and then one sperm can get through.

The eggs, whether fertilized or not, are moved through the Fallopian tubes down into the uterus and there, if they have been fertilized, they become attached to the uterine lining (endometrium) and grow. If they have not joined with sperm already, they may meet them in their downward passage and, becoming fertilized, nest in the uterus.

Since ovulation does not occur before the middle of the acceptance period (which starts at the eighth or ninth day from the first showing of swelling of the vulva and bleeding), the ideal time to mate dogs is close to ovulation, either a day before, or any time during the rest of the period. The fragile sperm do not live more than three days in the female tract, and perhaps are not able to fertilize when they are more than two. This is the reason why bitches mated the first day they will take the dog so often fail to become pregnant: the sperm cannot live until the eggs have been discharged from their follicles.

As soon as the follicles rupture, the pits made by this phenomenon fill with blood, thus forming bloody plugs called the blood bodies (*corpora hemorrhagica*). These soon change their characteristics and secrete a hormone, the luteal hormone, whose effect is almost opposite from that of the follicular hormone. The blood bodies become quite tough and, since they take up yellow stain when prepared for study, are called the luteal bodies. These *corpora lutea* persist during pregnancy and for some time thereafter.

The luteal hormone puts the brakes on the whole mating

cycle. Shortly after the luteal hormone enters the blood stream, the bitch's vulva, which has become firm and greatly swollen, loses its firmness, and within 36 hours becomes flabby and soft. If you own a Cocker bitch but have failed to note her first day, perhaps even being appraised of her condition by the actions of your male dogs or of neighbors' dogs camping on your lawn, then watch for this sudden softening of the vulva. It means she has ovulated, and that you had better not delay many days before mating her.

When she has conceived, in other words when the male sperm and eggs have joined and a new pup has been started, the egg with its complete pairs of chromosomes divides into two. Each of the daughter cells formed from the fertilized egg has complete pairs of chromosomes. This process of cell division continues until about the sixth, when one pair of cells is set apart to become the germ plasm of the pup.

The dividing cells become a hollow globe, which finally pulls in one side, just as if you let the air out of a hollow rubber ball and pushed one side of it in until it touched the other side, then squeezed it together until you made a canoe-shaped body, squeezing further until the two gunwales of the canoe touched and stayed together. What was the outside of the ball is now its inside.

This new formation grows and grows by cell division, until by the twenty-second day it is a very tiny object surrounded by protective coverings and the placenta, which connects it to the uterus. If you have a delicate sense of touch, you can feel it through the abdominal wall. You must put your thumb on one side of the Cocker's belly, your fingers on the other side, and, feeling very gently, you will discover several lumps as large as that shown in the diagram, and marked 22. They feel like tiny marbles, round and uniform.

By the twenty-fourth day they will be noticeably larger, and the diagram shows how large they will feel to you up to the thirty-fifth day. After that the lumps will be so soft that they will be difficult to feel, but one scarcely needs to anyway, because the size of the belly is a good indication.

If your bitch ovulates and does not conceive because she was not bred, the stud was sterile, or the mating took place too early, she will develop enlarged breasts, an increased appetite, and, 60 to 63 days from the time she ovulated, she will go through most of the activity of a bitch about to whelp, yet not produce pups. She may steal other pups to mother; she may produce some milk, so don't think she is sick. Rather, if she does not do these things, consider the probability that she did not ovulate. She will not retain the *corpora lutea* and may come in heat two months earlier than you expect.

In the days when Carré's disease was the great scourge of dogs it was very common to find bitches pregnant at the time they contracted the disease resorbing their puppies. I reported this fact many years ago in a veterinary journal. The interesting thing was that when the bitches did this, the pregnancy protected them against the disease, so that its effects were so mild one often would not normally know they were sick. This accounted for the survival of many more bitches than dogs in epizootics of that horrible disease.

Have you ever listened to discussions among dog breeders on whether to breed a bitch on her first, second, or third heat? If not, then if you are at all scientifically minded, get such an argument started and sit back and listen. I have done it many times, to learn all the ideas dog breeders have. In every such discussion the ideas most often expressed are based on thoughts about human beings. An adroit *why* interjected here and there soon brings out the fact that nearly all of the ideas are also based on rationalization and not knowledge. Here are some:

"You wouldn't want to see a thirteen-year-old girl have a baby, would you?" Answer: a thirteen-year-old girl is not grown or physically mature when she first menstruates; a bitch doesn't come in heat until she is mature. Time of marriage is a social convention. Moreover, a woman obstetrician tells us that the thirteen-year-old girls she has delivered have had their babies much more easily than older women.

"Puppies from older bitches will be better puppies than those from young ones." Anyone who makes this claim should present evidence, and all scientific studies show it to be without foundation. Many champions have come from bitches bred their first heats. Those who support the view with arguments should realize that they are also supporting the argument for the inheritance of acquired characteristics, a viewpoint pretty well vitiated by research. It is probably true that one can find more champions from the second heats of bitches than from the first, but this is because many breeders skip breeding the first heat through mistaken notions.

"A bitch isn't old enough to take proper care of puppies before she is two years old." More rationalizing. True, she may take better care of her second litter because of experience, but that is a very different matter. Mother love in a bitch is based on hormone production—prolactin. The second litter is no longer novel to her. She may take better care of her fourth. On the basis of the above argument she should never have her first litter.

The scientifically minded dog breeder wants to know why, and when he inquires of those with experience, he learns that many Cocker breeders have found (that a bitch bred her first litter) may have better spring of ribs than one bred later, because while her bones are "less brittle" they are pushed outward and tend "to set that way." How much of fact or fancy there is in this idea we do not know from research, but it is the opinion among a wide segment of Cocker fanciers who breed their bitches the first heat on this account, and find it does them no harm.

The person with an open mind also asks those who, like myself, have bred dogs in studies, and learns that we always breed the first heat and have had no bad results. I bred a Bloodhound bitch at five months of age (using hormones to bring her in heat). She raised a fine litter, and eventually grew to be a large bitch, but not quite so large as her litter mates.

Then there is another point too often overlooked, namely the possible loss of unique, valuable germ plasm which a puppy may carry. Dogs are subject to so many perils that their average age is probably not over five, and it is best to have litters as early as possible to be sure of getting any.

Besides, where space is limited it pays a breeder to know what kind of puppies a dog produces, so he can keep the best producers and eliminate the inferior. Why keep a bitch an extra year to find this out?

Many breeders owning valuable bitches have one or more miss, and want to have pups from them. Or certain bitches fail to come into heat, and the breeder wants to bring them in. This may be done with hormones, but it is a veterinary matter. In the Whitney Veterinary Clinic we have tried many drugs or combinations of drugs. The combination which has produced best results in bringing a bitch into heat is Stilbestrol. It may be given in pill form, or right in the food, or it may be injected. After about five days' treatment with five milligrams a day, a Cocker bitch will be in heat. After she comes in heat, two milligrams a day will continue the heat normally, but she probably will not ovulate. To produce ovulation we inject her with about 20 units of pregnant mare serum and breed her the next day. Our percentage of fertile matings has been high.

Chapter 9

REPRODUCTION IN THE MALE COCKER

In the preceding chapter we discussed the part the female plays in reproduction, and mentioned the sperm from the male. These very minute bodies are actually shaped like polliwogs. They are oval and flattish, each having a tail about nine times as long as the body. Each sperm, as we have seen, has half the normal complement of chromosomes.

Sperm—short for *spermatozoa*—are manufactured by the germ plasm of the dog, and this basic mass of cells is part of the *testicles.* The testicles are, in many ways, interesting organs.

They develop within the puppy's body but move outward through slits in the abdominal wall, and are already out of the body and just forward of the sac which holds them later—the *scrotum*—at the time of birth. Sometimes people who should know better compare the descent of the puppy testicles with those of boys', whose testicles do not descend until puberty, but there is no real basis for comparison.

While we are on this subject, we should know the terms which are used for the conditions in which the testicles fail to descend at all. When they remain in the abdomen, or when they have come through the abdominal rings but have not progressed far enough to occupy the scrotum, the condition is called *cryptorchism.*

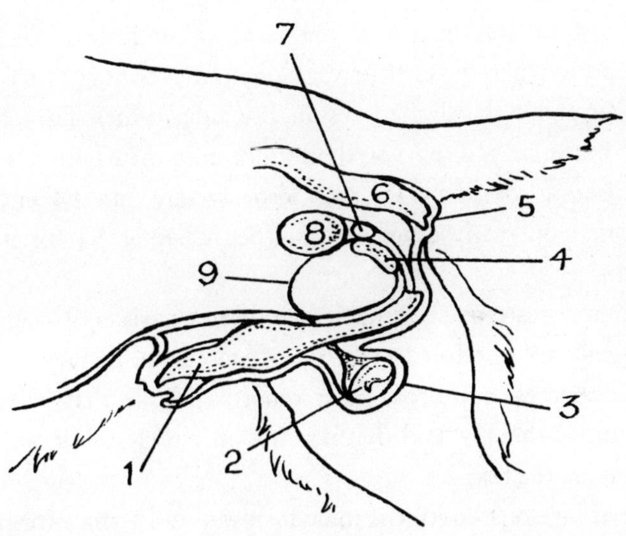

Male organs of reproduction. Reproductive system and neighboring organs of a dog. (1) Penis. (2) Testicle. (3) Scrotum. (4) Pelvis. (5) Anus. (6) Rectum. (7) Prostate. (8) Bladder. (9) Vas deferens.

A *monorchid* is a dog which has only one testicle, or a dog in which only one testicle has grown into the scrotum.

An *anorchid* is a dog without testicles, or one in which the testicles have not grown into the scrotum.

The word *grown* here may puzzle some readers who have the idea that testicles simply slide down a passageway into a sac.

Not at all. The process is one of growth. The testicle, while inside the abdomen, becomes adhered to the tissue lining the adbomen—the *peritoneum*. This then grows downward through the abdominal slits (rings), and drags the testicle with it. This growth is under the influence of a hormone made by the anterior pituitary gland. It is now manufactured synthetically, and sold under such terms as A.P.L. (anterior pituitary like). If this is injected early in the growth period into a cryptorchid puppy, it often stimulates the descent and renders him normal. In some older pups, when the testicle was close to the scrotum, it has also brought about the desired result. But dogs which have to be treated thus can still pass on the condition to their pups, and are bad risks as breeders. Cryptorchism is rare in Cockers, far rarer than in many other breeds. (See Chapter VI for its inheritance.)

When testosterone was first offered veterinarians, it was used repeatedly in an effort to correct cryptorchism, and several reports of success appeared. Later reports indicate that its use is substitutive therapy, and that it is not only useless, but tends to degenerate the testicles.

Sperm are of two kinds: male-forming and female-forming. This capacity is due to the number of chromosomes the sperm possess. Bitches have only one kind of chromosomes, but in male dogs a pair of them differ. One is called the X and the other the Y. And this is the explanation of sex, for when a male with a Y chromosome combines with an egg possessing a Y, the product is a bitch pup. When the X chromosome combines with a Y chromosome, the pup will be a male.

So theoretically there should be an equal number of dog and bitch pups born, but there are not. There are many more males than females. Those interested in following this study further can consult my book *How to Breed Dogs.* Conceptions occurring in the cold months result in a much higher ratio of males to females. There are influences at work—which we do not as yet understand—modifying the expectancy. But today we have no way of producing sex to order.

The male's testicles are outside the body because the heat inside would prevent the production of sperm. A muscle pulls them close to the body to keep them warm in cold weather and lengthens to permit movement of air and some sweating from the scrotum in hot weather.

The penis of members of the dog family is unique in that, besides being capable of becoming enlarged with blood, it has an area which enlarges much more than the forepart does. When there is no enlargement of the penis, it is quite small. The dog's penis contains a pointed bone which may be felt in the front part, and just behind this bone is located the section capable of great enlargement. When the dog copulates with a bitch, the penis is thrust into the vagina, where it instantly swells. The huge enlargement of the bulbous part takes place due to its filling with blood, and it becomes at least three times as large as the rest of the penis. In this way the dog is tied to the bitch; it is entirely due to the male, the bitch having no part in the initial tieing.

When tieing has occurred, the semen is pumped by spurts into the vagina. Probably then the bitch helps keep the penis enlarged, because there begins a series of peristaltic waves, which causes a slight tightening and relaxing of the vagina. Some Cocker males will remain tied (or hung) for five minutes, some for 60. A five-minute tie is just as satisfactory as a longer one, because the semen has been moved up through the uterus and Fallopian tubes to the ovarian capsules by the end of five minutes.

How often may a vigorous stud be bred without harm? Probably once a day will not hurt him. The week before he died, at thirteen years of age, Red Brucie bred seven bitches, all of which conceived. Nature is most generous with sperm. In one good mating a dog may discharge millions, and a copious sperm swarm be produced by dogs frequently mated. Rams offer an excellent example of the possibilities, for a single ram has been known to impregnate sixty ewes within 24 hours. I have seen a vigorous Cocker stud, left with a bitch, copulate five times with her, and remain tied at least 18 minutes each time. The dog showed no sign of weakness. It probably harms the dog not at all, but more than one breeding a day would produce questionable results in the ensuing litters. Some stud-dog owners refuse to permit their dogs to be bred more often than once a week, surely on sentimental, not on scientific, grounds.

Chapter 10

REARING COCKER PUPPIES

At the end of her gestation period the expectant Cocker mother lets you know that she will soon deliver her puppies. You can tell by such behavior as this: she seeks a nest. It may be a hole she digs in the ground, or her kennel bedding may be scratched up and rearranged. If she is a house dog, she may push your shoes together in a corner. If she is loose, you may find her in a secluded corner of your garden. She plainly shows that she wants to be by herself. If you wait for her to have her puppies and then move her to a place of your liking, she may turn against her pups. Even the best mothers become poor ones when disturbed during the first week after whelping.

Just before she whelps, a Cocker bitch's hair can be clipped from her breasts to good advantage. If she has been allowed to lie in a run infested with worm eggs, she may have thousands of them stuck to her nipples and to the waxy secretions on the skin. If she is thoroughly cleaned a day or two before she whelps, it may prevent early infestation of her pups by intestinal parasites, and thus remove one obstacle to raising the litter.

Cockers are amazingly good mothers. It is seldom necessary to help them, but when you see a bitch straining and accomplishing nothing for several hours, a call to your veterinarian is in order. The average Cocker will require about three hours to complete her whelping, but if she has a pup every 90 minutes, or takes six or eight hours to complete the task, it is not necessarily abnormal. A tiny amount (1/10 c.c.) of Pitocin injected under her skin will hurry a slow whelper remarkably.

If she fails to chew off a sac in which a puppy is born, you must rupture it and slip it off the pup, folding it back over the umbilical cord so she can consume it along with the placenta. She will do as well if you cut the cord off an inch from the puppies and dispose of the placenta as if she were permitted to be natural and eat it. There is doubt that she obtains anything of value from it. Very likely it is a holdover from the days when bitches were their own janitors and kept the nests clean in this way, just as they do when they consume the urine and feces of their puppies.

In this matter of elimination by puppies, it is not generally understood that they tend to hold their urine and feces until the lapping of the mother's tongue causes a relaxation of the sphincters. Persons rearing orphan puppies can keep their boxes perfectly clean by simply wiping the pups with a most piece of cotton until they eliminate.

When the pups are five or six days old their tails may be cut. You can do this, or have your veterinarian do it. If it is done properly, there is no need for stitching. Most breeders simply use a knife and, holding the tail over a block of wood, make an incision straight across it, at the point where the tail starts to become thinner. Every Cocker pup's tail has parallel sides for about three eighths of its length, and then it starts to taper. That is the place to cut. Most novices cut off too much, leaving only a button. The tail, when the pup is grown, should be just long enough to be even with a line projected upward from the

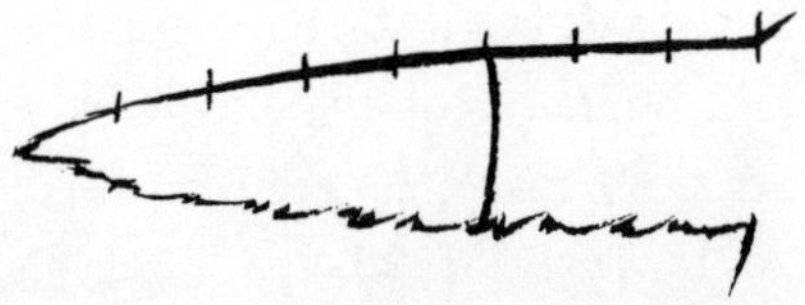

Where to cut a Cocker puppy's tail.

backs of the legs from hocks downward, which in turn should be perpendicular to the ground.

The extra digits on the rear feet—equivalent to the human thumbs—are called dewclaws, as has been mentioned in Chapter VII. In Cockers used for retrieving in water they are useful, but in pets and Cockers used only for upland bird hunting they are often a source of trouble. This is due principally to the fact that the nails do not reach the ground to wear off, and so may grow in a circle and penetrate the toe.

Only a small percentage of Cockers possess them anyway, and they are inherited (see Chapter VI), so may easily be bred out of a strain. If your pups are born with dewclaws which you feel will never be useful to the grown dog, trim them or have them trimmed off at the time the tails are docked.

Occasionally a bitch will lap a puppy's newly cut tail and keep it bleeding until she may weaken it greatly. Remember that there is almost a complete absence of iron and some other minerals in bitches' milk, a puppy being born with all he will have until he begins to eat solid food. If he hemorrhages early in life, his precious iron and sodium won't stretch out enough to enable him to live, and he will either be unthrifty or die.

The first food other than milk which puppies receive, if their mothers behave normally, will be partially digested stomach

Removing puppy dewclaws.
Should be done before sixth day with manicuring scissors, or left to veterinarian.

contents. The wild bitch kills rodents or obtains other food, comes home with it, digesting it as she comes, and then vomits among her litter of pups. They wallow in it, eating all they can. When they are done, she eats the remainder and laps them clean.

So, if your Cocker bitch acts doglike and unhumanly, don't imagine she is sick, but accept her actions as natural. You'd be amazed to know how many experienced breeders have brought bitches that behaved in this manner to veterinarians, because they thought the dogs were sick.

In Chapter XII you will learn about parasites. But here a warning: puppies can be and often are born infested. The embryonic worms remain dormant until birth, when they start to grow, and by three weeks of age the pups may be so anemic from loss of blood to hookworms, or so poisoned from roundworm toxins, that they succumb.

There is no harm done to three-week-old puppies by deworming if it is done properly. I deworm all of mine then, and again eleven or twelve days later, and have reduced puppy mortality a great deal in this way. In Chapter XII the safe doses are given. But if your pup is anemic and weak from worms, no dose is entirely safe. Don't blame the drug or the method then, but blame yourself for permitting the ravages of worms so to weaken your pups. If you find the pups prostrate after deworming, give them heat and it may revive them. Starvation is extremely necessary, because tetrachlorethylene is soluble in fat, and since bitches' milk is half fat, unless rigid starvation has preceded the drug, you can kill pups with it. But no method I know is so efficient or harmless when properly used.

Weaning is a crucial time in all puppies' lives, and it is a good time to commence weighing your pups to determine whether their growth is satisfactory. By all means start to wean them, and at the same time start to spare their mother, as soon as you can get your pups to eat. By using the right foods, this can be as early as 15 or 16 days.

Experience has shown that puppies do best on rich milk, to which foods containing good-quality protein and some minerals are added. If no Jersey milk is available, add some coffee cream to evaporated milk. And whatever you do, try to modify cows' milk toward bitches' milk, and not toward human milk, as we mentioned in Chapter IV. Almost all of the older books gave us formulae for simulated human milk, whereas bitches' milk is the very reverse. This table shows the difference:

TABLE II

THE DIFFERENCE IN COMPOSITION IN BITCH, COW, AND HUMAN MILK

	Bitch	*Cow*	*Human*
Water	77.0	86.3	87.3
Protein	7.3	3.5	1.3
Sugar	3.7	4.7	7.5
Fat	11.0	4.0	3.5

Instead of adding dextrose (glucose) and lime water, we must add more fat and more protein, and subtract sugar. Dextrose is a sugar, as is lactose, which is milk sugar. Puppies have been raised on such improper diets, but not nearly so well as on one such as this:

Lactogen	2 oz. by volume.
Heavy cream (30 per cent butterfat)	2 oz. by volume.
Water	4 oz. by volume.

If you make such a mixture, the sugar in the lactogen will be a little higher than the ideal, but I have raised hundreds of pups on it, and so have our clients. Now don't spoil it, when the pups are old enough to eat solid food, by adding baby cereals to it. Remember that babies require seventeen years to grow, whereas puppies have explosive growth—your Cocker pup will be grown in seven months. There are excellent puppy meals to be had, designed for rapid puppy growth and containing all the necessary minerals and vitamins, besides the complete proteins and fats which the explosive growth of puppies requires. Pampa was the first such food. It is reliable and pups like it. I often start sixteen-day-old puppies on it, and I find it makes a truly excellent weaning food. For those selling

Three generations of champions, all in their natural coats.

puppies, such a food is a godsend, because a small supply may be given or sold with each puppy, which foresight upon your part prevents digestive upsets. You will find that many buyers return puppies to you because of loose stools, which are due only to change of diet. It is well to have the buyer continue on the food your puppies have been eating. If that can be arranged, one source of worry will have been banished.

Some puppy sellers give with each puppy a stupid yet elaborate set of feeding instructions embodying the feeding of a great variety of foods, and causing a lot of trouble in preparation. These lists are entirely unnecessary, and simply show the buyer that you are a generation behind the times in your knowledge of dog feeding. Science has demonstrated that all this fuss is absurd, and that a high-grade meal food, plus fat and milk for the young pup, will do a better job, and that variety is not necessary.

As the puppy grows, you may note a small lump over the umbilicus or navel. A high percentage of Cockers fail to heal across completely, and the bulge you feel is a hernia. In such a slight deformity there is no danger unless the opening through the abdomen is sufficiently large to permit a loop of intestine to work out into the sac you feel. If it is small, the sac will eventually harden into a lump which never harms the dog and, since the Cocker has long hair, is not noticeable. If the orifice is large enough to allow the intestine to work through, have your veterinarian repair it before a strangulation occurs.

At very close to fourteen weeks of age the two upper middle incisors will loosen and be pushed out by a new pair. Then the teeth will gradually all fall out and be replaced. If, at this crucial time, the puppy has any sickness which disturbs his metabolism, the enamel will not be deposited on the teeth. If they are partway in, you will eventually find a ring around the teeth. If the sickness occurred earlier, only the tips of the teeth may be pitted and discolored. It used to be thought that only "distemper" caused such disfigurement, but today we know better; many ailments can cause it.

In Chapter XIII we shall consider vaccinations against various diseases, so we need not go into the problem here.

The American Kennel Club insists upon litter registrations before the individual puppies of the litter may be registered. Since this process requires several weeks, it is well to send the application, properly filled out, to the A.K.C. and have the litter registration in your hands by the time the puppies are old enough to sell. You can thus be ready to give each buyer a com-

Nonquitt Notable—a great asset to Cockerdom.

pleted individual registration application with the litter number on it. This foresight, too, saves headaches.

It is highly important to sell your pups at as early an age as possible, because you will get no more for them once they are out of the cute puppy stage than you will when they are seven weeks old, and often less. So advertising should be planned well in advance to appear at the proper time. Newspaper ads seldom bring the buyers willing to pay what those who read the national magazines will pay—expect to pay. In the former case you will answer many phone calls from those wanting $5.00 pups; in the latter, there will be voluminous correspondence from those who want to know the ancestry back to Obo II.

Have some photos of the parents and the litter if possible. This will save hours of writing.

Chapter 11

EARLY TRAINING

"As the twig is bent, so is the tree inclined" is only partly true in dog training. A tree, once it inclines, remains that way, but an animal's mind, once it gets untrained by a long period of non-use, can be re-educated nicely. It is amazing how quickly and well little puppies can be trained in useful ways in the first place.

Even though I have considered training in some detail in later chapters, the principles of early training are so vital that I have thought it worth-while to call your attention to the most basic of them before proceeding any further.

Housebreaking is one of the main concerns. A puppy eliminates in response to the feel of what he stands on. If he first does so on the wire of a wire-bottomed pen, he will more than likely do so subsequently on the grating of a one-pipe furnace if he can find one. If he learns first on newspaper, he will try to find that, and if he learns on a clipped lawn, he will sense that your rug with the deepest nap is the proper place to relieve himself.

Cocker breeders often raise pups in a pen the bottom of which is covered with straw. Is it any wonder, therefore, that a pup whose only strawy environment is his new dog house with its straw bottom will soil only that? To make the buyer realize that he is getting an easily housebroken dog, start your pups on newspaper, and explain to the prospective buyer how to housebreak. When the puppy, in his new home, has become accustomed to using the paper spread on the kitchen floor, explain how it must be moved by stages out on to the back lawn or wherever it is desired to have the dog eliminate, how the pup should be taken out after meals when it normally feels the urge, and how the whole thing is a matter of habit formation, that the exceptions are serious, and how, if a puppy be given the opportunities he needs, there will be few failures.

Prospective buyers admire the response of young puppies to commands. You can teach them what *go in the house* means, and to come to a whistle, the word *come,* or the clapping of your hands. Use the word *come* distinctly as you shoo them into their house, or when you call them out to feed them. It does not require very many repetitions of the word to establish a conditioned reflex, and the word will have a meaning.

Only a minutely small percentage of Cockers are ever field trained, but I feel sure that if more owners knew the fun they are missing by never giving their dogs a chance at their work, many Cockers would be well field trained. Even ten-week-old puppies will show interest in bird work and retrieving. It pays well to be able to demonstrate these early aptitudes to prospective buyers. Only a few minutes a day need be spent in rolling a ball for puppies to chase and catch. Once they start this, it is easy to train them, one at a time, to drop the ball in your hand or at your feet (see Chapter XV).

At the tender age of four weeks every puppy in a litter can be standing like a rock in a show position. Indeed this is the best age to start them. A connoisseur can make a fairly accurate appraisal of the best of any litter by this early posing and training, and the pups enjoy it.

A small tidbit given at the conclusion of the posing session will help you establish the pattern. With one of your fingers under the puppy's jaw and another under his tail, the puppy will stand as if hypnotized for some minutes. Examine his mouth, and don't let him win should he resist your efforts. End each training period by showing him that you and your hands are much stronger than he is, and that you are boss.

I am often amazed at how ineffectual many people are. Almost unable, apparently, to use their hands enough to force a puppy to their will, these persons will complain, "If I discipline him, he comes right at me and bites." Some Cockers are thus trained to be ugly. Why, the weakest woman could easily kill a half-grown Cocker pup with her bare hands. Poor training cannot be excused by saying, "I can't." What it really means is, "I won't try."

A puppy which is made to submit to human beings, and which acknowledges early in his life that they are his superiors, will usually remain tractable throughout his existence, unless he possesses inherited meanness—an unreliable temperament. Even such puppies can be trained to be more reliable, but they should not be used for breeding.

If you breed and sell Cockers for hunting, then there is less need to try to sell them as cute puppies, but more need to develop their hunting characteristics. As you will see in Chapter XV, your puppies must mind instantly, and show bird sense. Nearly all Cockers do show bird sense, but minding is a matter of training. Read Chapter VII and there you will get some ideas about how to develop both the pup's bird sense and, to some degree, his minding while he is yet fairly young. Puppies trained even partially will command double the price of those simply allowed to age.

Chapter 12

YOUR COCKER'S HEALTH—PARASITES

Trying to compress all you need to know about the ailments of dogs into a couple of chapters means omitting a great deal of interest to every dog owner. A whole book, written by my son and myself, called *The Distemper Complex,* treats quite adequately what we know about only eleven diseases. Another I wrote, called *The Complete Book of Dog Care,* covers all of the common ailments, and makes one realize how all but impossible it is to do justice to the subject here. So we shall treat only matters of paramount importance.

There's an old adage among entomologists that it's no disgrace to get a bug, it's only a disgrace to keep it. It seems to me that there should be another phrase with this, to the effect that when dealing with our dogs it is also a disgrace to allow the dog to become reinfested. And incidentally, while we're talking about parasites, the word is *infest,* not *infect.*

Insects, intestinal worms, and protozoa (single-cell animals) all affect Cockers at some time of their lives, and some unfortunate dogs harbor a few throughout their entire lives. Unless we know the life histories of the common parasites of Cocker Spaniels, we are not going to be able to control them as we should, for while we may give remedies which destroy the parasites, that is no guarantee that they will not reinfest the dog, and we shall have to do it all over again many times.

THE DOG FLEA

The little black insects that jump, sometimes landing on one's ankle or calf, are either male or female. After they have become mature, the males remain little, but the females develop rather long, brownish-yellow bodies which are filled with eggs. These eggs are dropped about the premises wherever the dog happens to be, and they may roll into cracks in the floor, or in the nap of rugs, or even around in the buttons of an overstuffed chair. They are often called sand fleas, because they are found so often in sandy places, which form an excellent environment for their development.

This, in general, is the life history of the flea. The eggs, as I have said, roll off the dog, and this may go on throughout the whole year. But the eggs do not develop until the weather becomes warm and damp, when they absorb moisture, and the little larvae inside grow and finally hatch as worms. So the first stage of the flea after the egg stage is a worm. It crawls about eating organic matter such as scales from dog skin, certain forms of dust, dog hair, etc., and when it has become a little more than an eighth of an inch long, it spins a cocoon and pupates, just as does a caterpillar in turning into a butterfly.

When the flea hatches, it crawls up anything that happens to lead upward, such as the leg of a chair, a piece of grass, or the stem of a bush. There it waits, about six inches to a foot from the ground, until something moves past it. It might be your dog or your ankle at which it jumps—and it can jump enormous distances in proportion to its size. If it is the dog on which it alights, it will probably stay there the rest of its life, mate, and, if it is a female, produce eggs which fall off again to complete another life cycle.

There are four common types of fleas which infest dogs: the human flea, the dog flea, the cat flea, and the stick-tight flea. Human fleas prefer human beings, but will breed on the dog. The dog and cat fleas infest either dogs or cats, and will jump on to human beings, but, because they are so choosy, will jump off them on to the first dog or cat they can find. The stick-tight flea is often found around the rims of the dog's ears but may sometimes attach to other parts of the body. If you own a Cocker, your problem will be almost entirely with the dog flea, which is found particularly as the weather gets damp. In some states of the United States there are no fleas, because the climate is too dry for them to develop.

Stick-tight fleas differ in their life history from the other types. They cling to the skin, sometimes in large clusters. The female burrows into the skin and lays her eggs in little ulcers which she produces. Then, after the eggs hatch, the larvae fall to the ground, where they develop for about four weeks. You find stick-tight fleas more often in warm than in cold climates, and they are to be found on several species of animal, even birds. You must not take the colloquial term "stick-tight" always to denote a flea; sometimes, and in some areas, the word applies only to ticks.

Treatment for the control of fleas is very easy. It takes many forms, one of which, of course, is to prevent the dog from contacting fleas, that is, keeping him out of places known to be infested. The second method is to kill all fleas on the dog. This may be done in many ways. The modern sprays kill them effectively, and leave some residue. The powders on the market are also excellent, and usually last for at least a week. They need not be dusted all over the dog, because fleas move about him all day, and it is only necessary to cover a large spot on the back and perhaps on the chest. Another method is the use of a good rinse. This is applied simply by giving the dog a bath, squeezing out all the water after the soap has been rinsed from his coat, and then adding about a teaspoonful of dip or rinse to a quart of water. An emulsifying agent in it causes the killing material, which is in oily form, to spread through the solution, giving it a milky appearance. The solution is poured all over the dog, and every flea it touches will be destroyed. This is a very effective remedy, but it does not leave so long lasting a residue as the powder or sprayed material.

Hardly a day goes by all summer when we at the Whitney Veterinary Clinic do not have an inquiry on these lines: "I've just returned from vacation, and the house is alive with fleas." This happens in the very best families, but with the proper knowledge it can easily be corrected. What it means is that while the family was away the flea eggs left by dogs or cats have hatched, the larvae have pupated and are waiting for something live to jump upon.

To cure this condition, it is simply necessary to get a good spray in the form of an Aerosol bomb. Start at one corner of the infested room and spray so that a mist is left about a foot from the floor; back away from it as you spray the room. Then close the door and you will find that all the fleas will die during the few minutes you are absent from the room.

Another method of control is to dust your dog heavily with a good flea-killing powder and turn him loose in any infested room. As he runs around, the fleas will jump on him and commit suicide by getting into the powder.

Flea powders are so inexpensive today, and so effective, that it's hardly worth-while trying to make your own. Many of them now contain a fungicide which not only kills fleas, but prevents summer fungus from occurring, and I think this is the best treatment you can give your Cocker. It was my own discovery, and naturally I feel proud to know that so many million dogs have not had to scratch since it has been on the market. The discovery was given to the world by my publication in *Veterinary Medicine Magazine*.

THE LOUSE

In contrast to the life of the flea, that of the dog louse, both embryonic and adult, is on the animal. It depends on the animal for its meals, and a louse which is off the coat for more than three days dies. You will find several kinds of lice on Cockers at one time or another. I've seen a great many. Some are blue, some red, and some gray, but their life histories are all quite similar. Some live by sucking, and some by biting and chewing the skin of the dog. The life history of the louse proceeds in this order. First the female louse passes an egg, a nit, which the female fastens to a hair. The little sucking louse fastens itself on to the body of the dog by its mouth, and from then on it sucks blood and stays very close to the same spot. A great many lice will suck so much blood from a dog that they can make it anemic and even kill it. I have seen many dogs killed by sucking lice. On the other hand, the biting louse, while it annoys the dog and makes him scratch terribly, does not live on blood but on the scales from the skin; it also moves around, while the sucking louse does not. The female biting louse also attaches eggs to the dog hairs. All louse eggs appear oval shaped and almost silvery, especially if you use a reading glass to magnify them.

When a nursing bitch has lice, you will find that they tend to leave her for her puppies. In general, lice are spread from one dog to another by contact, and not by eggs. Only dogs that are kept close together or which have the opportunity to rub against one another contract these insects.

When little puppies become infested with the bloodsucking type of lice, they lose so much blood that they die in a short time. It is remarkable how frequently the owners of ailing puppies never think of looking at their skins to see if they are harboring parasites.

When dogs scratch, they loosen the lice and scratch them off. This applies even to the sucking lice, but then if another dog lies on the spot where the louse is, it will become infested. Scratching is an excellent sign that one should look a dog over for lice. Infestation occasionally escapes even veterinarians, because the insects may be so few and far between that even a very careful examination will fail to discover them. Then a week or two later, when a large crop of nits have hatched, it will be very simple to find them. If you suspect your Cocker of having lice, look in the ears and particularly examine the hairs, because for some reason lice seem to thrive among the long hairs of these dogs, and you will find the silvery eggs attached to the hairs even before you are able to locate the lice themselves.

Treatment is the same as for the dog flea. But you must be

much more meticulous in seeing to it that every inch of the dog is covered by the drug you use to kill the insects, or some little area will escape and be an Achilles heel from which the dog will then become reinfested. What you must do is wait until the eggs have hatched but the young are not old enough to lay eggs themselves. This means that two dippings or two thorough applications of a good powder, eleven days apart, will take care of all the insects on a dog.

DOG TICKS

These nasty insects make the dog appear to be covered with animated beans. The ticks' heads are buried in the animal's skin. Perhaps you think they don't exist in your part of the country, and they may not at present, but you may find that within a number of years your district, too, has become filled with these obnoxious creatures. I can well remember when there were none in Connecticut so far as any of us knew but today there are parts of the state in which ticks are almost as common as they are in areas of the South. Long Island and Cape Cod, Massachusetts, are other heavily-infested areas. And we are hearing of ticks moving northward at an alarming rate.

There are many ticks which, in the course of their life history, live on dogs. There are dog ticks, wood ticks, spotted fever ticks, Pacific Coast ticks, brown dog ticks, Lone Star ticks, etc., etc. Certain ticks are known by a number of names, but the life histories of all of them are so similar that they may be regarded as one.

Ticks pass through four stages: egg, seed tick, nymph, and adult. When the egg hatches, the seed tick may live off any one of a number of animals—mice, rats, woodchucks, or any rodent. Finally it drops off, and after catching hold of another animal and becoming adult, it may manage to get on your Cocker and engorge itself with blood. The female becomes very large, and the tiny male lives just underneath her. In fact, you almost always find a male underneath the female.

An adult female tick, after she has dropped off the dog, may lay as many as 4,000 eggs, and it depends on what kind of tick it is whether your home will become infested or not. The brown dog tick prefers to spend its early life in dwellings, and you'll often find these inside picture mouldings, behind baseboards, and even in furniture. But this tick will not attack human beings: it prefers dogs. Many of the other ticks will attack human beings.

The seed ticks have six legs. After the seed tick has been carried around by a rodent for 2 to 10 days, during which it has engorged itself with blood, it then develops eight legs, and moults, and is called a nymph. When it manages to find another host, it again engorges itself with blood, drops off, and moults again. Now it is a mature tick, and when it is in the open it gravitates toward a path through the woods, where it finds a bush to climb, from which it can drop on your dog. No one knows how ticks seem to sense that they must find paths where animals are likely to pass, but it is a fact that many more of them are found in such places than in pathless woods. After the female has laid her eggs, she dies, and that ends the cycle.

If you see a dog scratching and find these bean-shaped ticks on him, look the dog over well for more of them, especially around the ears and head. You may find them actually inside the ear.

Treatment consists of either pulling them out with a pair of pincers, trying to pull the tick head out also, or putting a drop of kerosene on the tick. Some people have tried holding a hot match near the creature to force it to drop off.

But these are only retail ways of getting rid of the ticks. Wholesale destruction is much better. You can go into almost any pet shop today and buy tick remedies that do a wonderful job. They can be in the form of sprays, powders, or dips, but they are all much stronger than those designed to get rid of fleas or lice.

Prevention is important, too, so keep your Cockers out of the woods as much as possible during the time of year they are likely to become infested. Or, if you do have to take them into the woods, spray them afterward to get rid of any ticks while they are still tiny and before their heads have become embedded in the dogs' skin.

MANGE MITES

There are three kinds that affect Cockers—the red mange mite, the sarcoptic mange mite, and the ear mange mite. All are so small that one needs a microscope to distinguish them, although a person with exceptionally keen eyes can make out the whitish color of the ear mange mite.

The Red Mange Mite (called the demodectic or follicular mange mite)

This is a longish mite with eight pairs of legs, and it lives mostly in the hair follicles. When your dog shows a bare spot on the cheek, around the eyes, or on the short hair of the front leg, you should suspect red mange. Take the dog to the veterinarian, and if there is infestation he will show you the mites under the microscope. You will see newly hatched ones which look like mere globules of protoplasm and mature ones.

If the affected areas are not treated promptly they will

spread, the mites crawling out of one follicle or one sebaceous gland into another, increasing as they do so. One mite will have become twelve within eight days. Mites take a very short time to mature, so it is very easy to understand how they spread so alarmingly. The first mite that infests a dog will take a long time to become a thousand, but for that thousand to turn into twelve thousand takes the same time as it took one to become twelve, and so your dog seems to blossom out all at once.

It is very easy to kill red mange mites in the skin of dogs if the proper drug is used, and your veterinarian undoubtedly has it. In the Whitney Veterinary Clinic we use rotenone, because it has such a low toxicity, and the areas we treat are usually cured in a few days. The difficulty in curing red mange completely lies in not treating areas which one doesn't realize are infested, and you can remedy this by dusting the dog over with a good flea powder every few days. Then any mites that crawl out of follicles will be killed by it. If you do not do this, you will find that, while you have cured one place, there has been another incubating which you did not see, and by the time you have cured that, perhaps twenty other places will have appeared. However, I have cured dogs that were almost completely bald as a result of red mange, and have seen some very pathetic cases cured so that they never showed any infested areas again.

Red mange is not only harmful in itself but is hard on the dog because side infections manage to develop along with the mange mites, so that sometimes huge ugly sores appear on the dog, and these may not be directly caused by the mites at all. In this case a remedy that kills the mites will not cure the dog, and sometimes the use of antibiotics and fungicides forms an excellent adjunct to the mange cure.

Sarcoptic Mange Mites

These are among the commonest Cocker parasites, although they are frequently not suspected. I have seen kennels in which many of both the adult dogs and puppies were infected, while the owners thought there was a fungus disease present.

The mite is very different from the demodectic or red mange mite. This one is round and has four pairs of short legs, with long hairs protruding from its body. The female lays twenty to forty eggs, which she deposits in tunnels underneath the skin. These hatch in three to seven days, and one female can easily produce one and a half million descendants in three months. Only females burrow underneath the skin, males and immature forms living on the surface, under scabs or skin scales. That is one reason why the disease is so easy to control, provided one is not discouraged after seeing no results from one treatment.

This mange mite also attacks human beings, and it is quite necessary that both the dog and the human owner be treated at the same time, or it is not possible completely to overcome the infestation on the dog.

Almost any mild antiseptic that will kill the males will in time eradicate the disease, because as the new mites hatch and crawl out of the skin, they will be destroyed by it; but it must be applied quite frequently. Even lard and sulphur have been known to cure the condition, but of course there are many better remedies which your veterinarian can supply you. If you use an oily rotenone solution, it will kill the females in their tunnels under the skin because it penetrates to them, and the rotenone will not only kill the old females, but apparently destroys the eggs, too. I have seen just two applications of such a remedy completely cure a Cocker of sarcoptic mange.

If your dog has the disease, examine yourself and the other members of your family for reddish areas which itch. If you own a cat, it won't hurt to look at it, too. The standard remedy used on humans is lindane in a vanishing-cream base. One takes a bath, dries, and spreads the cream over the affected areas, one application usually being sufficient. This also works well on dogs, but no bath is necessary. And even the same ordinary rinse that is used to destroy fleas and lice, if it is used on dogs every day or so, will eventually cure sarcoptic mange.

The Ear Mange Mite

These little mites are roundish, and look something like the sarcoptic mites. They live in the ear canal and the hair just around the outside of the ear, and they cause a crumbly wax. One must be careful about symptoms here. A rather nasty odor sometimes exudes from the ear and may even be smelled before you realize the dog has anything wrong with it, but that is not an indication of ear mange mites. But if you look into the dog's ear, and he has been scratching it or shaking his head, and you find that the wax is dryish, light or dark gray, and scaly-looking, the chances are excellent that your Cocker is afflicted with ear mange mites. In that case, take some of the wax out, spread it on a piece of glass, and mix it with a little mineral oil. Then take a reading glass and look closely, and if there are mites you will actually be able to see them moving around like grains of dust, but they will be very small, and you will have to look very carefully to see them, even with eightfold magnification.

Treatment consists of putting into the ear any drug which will kill bugs without damaging the organ. A mild rotenone solution is excellent, and will cure the disease in one application. But you must remember that there are mites in the hair around the ear which, after the drug has gone, will migrate into the ear again. So it is generally necessary to give two or three applications of the drug about a week apart, and this will end the difficulty, usually for good.

Your veterinarian will give you an ear mite remedy of his choice, enough for the purpose. I strongly recommend that if you have a cat you look into the animal's ears, particularly if you see is shaking its head or scratching. If the cat harbors these mites it will only give them back to the dog, and you will have the whole treatment to repeat again and again.

RED BUGS OR CHIGGERS

Throughout much of the United States, the woods are full of a tiny bug, almost too small to see, which goes by a variety of names. Chigger and red bug are the chief, but in Mexico and some parts of the deep South you hear them called chigga or chigre, and in some places they are called harvest mites.

Few dog owners realize what a nuisance these can be to their pets. If you find that your Cocker has a lot of small red welts which cause him to scratch terribly the day after you have had him in fields or woods where red bugs are usually found, you may be sure they are the culprits. Only the larval stage of the parasite annoys our dogs. The larvae attach themselves to the skin, suck blood, and then drop off, but the place at which they attach is extremely itchy, not only during the short period of attachment, but for many days thereafter. There is usually nothing that can be done about it, and when the inflammation has subsided the itching stops.

Of course if you know that your dog has been exposed to places infested by red bugs a bath followed by a good rinse with rotenone or some other bug killer in the water will destroy all of them and prevent any irritation.

INTERNAL PARASITES

People have strange ideas about intestinal parasites of dogs. Some think we can immunize dogs against them. Others think that when the parasites have been removed that is the end of them. Yet others have the idea that when a dog reaches the age of a year he is no longer susceptible to internal parasites of any kind. The table below will disabuse the minds of any who entertain such beliefs. It was made by studies of more than 5,000 fecal examinations at the Whitney Veterinary Clinic. It is fairly representative of what one may expect in New England. By studying it, you will see that there is no time in a dog's life when he is immune to parasites, but in certain cases, such as coccidiosis, he is more likely to be infested when he is quite young. This is probably because all dogs, at one time or another, become infested and thereafter are no longer susceptible.

These percentages, obviously, do not necessarily apply in all parts of the country. We have had correspondence with veterinarians who have said that in their localities whipworms were almost unknown but were being introduced by dogs from other areas. Western kennels have been infested by dogs from the East, some told us. Be that as it may, the table does show that dogs are not immune, at any time of life, from any of the common parasites except the coccidium.

Estimated Probability of Intestinal Parasite Infestation at Any Age by Per Cent*

AGE	ROUNDWORMS	HOOKWORMS	WHIPWORMS	TAPEWORMS FLEA-HOST	TAPEWORMS RABBIT-HOST	COCCIDIOSIS RIVOLTA	COCCIDIOSIS BIGEMINA	COCCIDIOSIS FELIS
0–3 weeks	40	20	0	3	0	0	0	8
4–11 weeks	50	20	5	9	1	9	1	7
12–23 weeks	42	20	10	10	1	6	1	5
24–51 weeks	27	20	25	14	1	3	2	3
1 year	17	20	28	14	3	2	3	3
2 years	16	20	30	14	5	2	1	2
3 years	15	20	30	14	4	2	1	1
4 years	14	20	30	14	4	2	1	1
5 years	13	20	30	14	3	2	0	1
6 years	12	20	30	14	2	2	0	1
7 years	11	20	30	14	1	1	0	0
8 years	10	20	30	14	0	1	0	0
9 years	9	20	30	14	0	1	0	0
10–15 years	8	20	30	14	0	1	0	0

*Based on a study by the author of four thousand fecal examinations of Connecticut dogs.

Whipworms

Since whipworm infestation in the mature dog stands first on our list, we will consider it first. What applies to other breeds applies equally to Cockers.

The whipworm is a small creature about half an inch long having a threadlike whip attached to the end of its body. The whip is sewed into the intestine lining, and from it the worm hangs, living on food which it takes from the dog's intestine. The worm gives off a severe toxin, or poison. Little harm is done to the dog by the loss of food, but the poison is so virulent that it takes only a few whipworms to make a dog debilitated. When he first becomes infested, he shows it more than he does after he has been able to neutralize the toxin by means of antibodies developed in the blood.

Many ordinary worm capsules will destroy the whipworms in a dog's intestine, but because they do not reach the cecum, or blind gut, of the dog, large numbers of the worms often gather there and live their whole lives.

For some reason whipworms cause a dog's stools to be firm one day and very loose the next. They may even cause bleeding from the intestine, so the stools have a sort of raspberry-jam appearance. They also cause some dogs to have running fits, and many a fine hunting dog has been discarded simply because it was too difficult to remove the whipworms. For a long time veterinarians found it so difficult to remove the worms that they operated on dogs, removing the cecum and thus eliminating many of the worms.

This operation is completely unnecessary today, because, while it is slightly troublesome, it is not difficult to remove all the whipworms from any dog. I believe that every dog owner should have a fecal examination made of his dog every six months, and, whenever any unusual symptoms appear, have it done again. Then your veterinarian will be able to tell you whether your dog is infested or clean. But be sure he makes a centrifuge flotation examination or he may overlook whipworm eggs, which are extremely heavy, and unless the solution used to float them has a specific gravity of almost 1.4, they will settle to the bottom and be missed.

Whipworms lay lemon-shaped eggs which pass out with the stools. No one knows how long they may live in the soil, but it may be as much as five years. The dog, in some way, is directly infested by them, perhaps through inhaling dust which gets into the mouth, the contamination of food, licking the feet, or picking up stones in the dog run where whipworm eggs exist. The shell is digested off the egg and the little larva liberated. It moves down the intestine until it finds a place where it can sew its tiny whip under the lining, and there it lives. When it is grown, it lays eggs in amounts which are huge compared to its own size.

A number of treatments are recommended. My son and I developed one, and published a paper about it in *Veterinary Medicine Magazine*. I think it is the easiest to administer as well as the most effective and inexpensive home remedy. Starve the dog completely for 24 hours—*every* form of nourishment must be withheld. Now give the average Cocker one 2 c.c. capsule of normal butyl chloride. Wait one hour, and then give a second, continuing hourly until five have been given. Two hours later feed the dog. Give no physic whatever, and the worms will be easily removed without inconvenience to the dog. If you give all the capsules at one time, the dog is almost certain to regurgitate most of them, and the effect will be lost.

Your veterinarian can supply you with a drug called Whipcide, which is a prescription drug, but we feel that it is not so effective as the normal butyl chloride given as directed above.

The Roundworm

The roundworm grows to be about four or five inches long, and usually lives curled up in the intestine or in the stomach. It moves up and down the intestine, and sometimes a whole wad of them are found together. And sometimes they are found stretched out all along the intestine. Some are white and some yellowish white, and they are pointed at the ends.

These worms lay a prodigious number of eggs, which are passed out in the stools. The eggs will not incubate unless the temperature is fairly high, and they will lie for years in the soil, waiting for the dog to take them into his mouth in some way and swallow them. The dog digests off the cell, liberating the larva, which bores through into the lymph and blood and is floated around for several days, growing somewhat and then becoming caught in the lungs. It bores through from the blood side of the lungs to the air side, and is then worked upward into the windpipe, where the irritation causes the dog to gag, and it swallows the phlegm. The larva goes down the gullet into the intestine, and becomes an intestinal parasite.

Those who raise pups will want to know an additional feature of this worm. If a pregnant bitch is infested, the larvae in her blood will not be caught in the lungs as often as in the placenta. They bore through this and get to the puppies' blood, where they remain dormant until the puppies are born, when they begin to develop. This explains why young puppies can be so heavily worm-infested and shows how necessary it is to deworm them at a very early age. Similarly, it shows how vital it is to keep a bitch, from before she is bred till after her puppies have been weaned, in a perfectly worm-free environment, where there can be no eggs under any conditions.

As mentioned in the chapter on rearing puppies, it is also a good idea to clean the breasts of a bitch, because pups can often

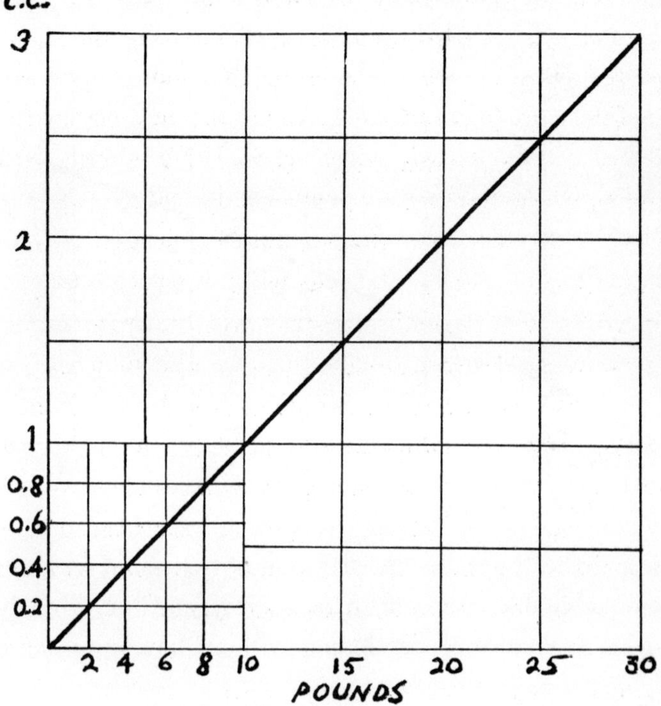

Safe doses of tetrachlorethylene for robust, empty Cockers.

find many worm eggs in the waxy secretions around a bitch's teats and on the breast itself.

Since in the study we made of puppies and their parasites we found that nearly all litters are infested with roundworms and many with hookworms, we now make it a practice to deworm all our puppies at three or four weeks of age, no matter how healthy they may seem. It must be remembered that the worm has to be several weeks old before it can lay eggs. You may have pups heavily infested with roundworms and yet a fecal examination will show no eggs whatsoever. Then, if this is done day after day, you may suddenly find thousands of eggs in the stools, because the worms have come of age and can now lay them. On this account it is not worth-while waiting to deter-

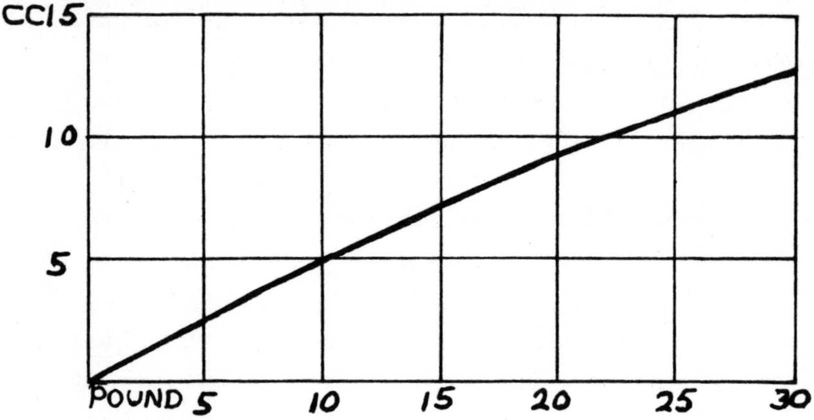

Safe doses of normal butyl chloride for robust, empty Cockers.

mine whether pups are infested or not. It is safer, and in my opinion advisable, to worm them anyway, and thus give them a far better chance of developing without having to contend with the toxins secreted by worms.

The curve on page 155 shows you the proper dosage for Cockers of any weight if you use tetrachlorethylene, the drug which is probably most effective. There is also a curve for the amount of N-butyl chloride, which is also extremely effective, but is slightly more toxic to tiny puppies than is tetrachlorethylene. In either case, the animal should be completely starved. Puppies should be starved for 18 to 20 hours, and grown dogs should be starved for 24 hours, which will do them no harm at all. One hour after the administration of the drug it is wise to physic the dog with a good tapeworm specific, such as arecolene hydrobromide (which will, of course, also remove tapeworms), or it can be just milk of magnesia, which is much slower-acting but is effective. If milk of magnesia is used, wait at least two hours before feeding the dog; after giving arecolene hydrobromide, however, you may feed it one hour after dosage, because it is a violent physic, usually removing tapeworms and clearing out the dog within 45 minutes. There are also other excellent worm medicines on the market, such as Caracide and hexylresorcinol, but they are no more effective and are more expensive.

A new worm killer may be administered along with your Cocker's food. As this is written several pharmaceutical companies are marketing it. Research indicates that it is quite safe and effective against the common roundworms but that it destroys only one form of hookworm, and that unfortunately is the type often found in dogs. This may be had at any drug store. The dose is indicated on the package and need not be as exact as some other drugs.

Hookworms

Hookworms are minute leeches which live by sucking blood from the intestine. They cling to it by teeth or hooks around the mouth—hence the name. Because they live on blood, they are deadly to little puppies. As we have seen previously, puppies cannot afford to lose iron from their blood; if much is lost, they die from anemia. Even grown dogs will lose much weight, have rather loose stools, and be generally out of condition with even a moderate infestation of hookworms.

The hookworm's life history is quite different from that of the roundworm. The size of the creatures is very dissimilar. The hookworm is not much more than half an inch long, the male being slightly smaller than the female, and both are about as thick as a piece of ordinary shoe thread, which makes it all the more amazing that they can do so much damage to our dogs. The eggs have to incubate for from three to six days, depending upon temperature, and then tiny larvae emerge; this is called the first larval stage. Three days later the larvae moult, becoming second-stage larvae. Eight days later they moult again, becoming third-stage or infective larvae, and lie waiting for a host. They can bore through the skin on the feet or the dog's body if they are not taken in through the mouth. Sometimes, in very severely infested runs, you will see big areas on a dog's sides from which the hair has fallen and which looks very red, through hookworm larvae having attacked the skin. But most larvae are probably ingested through the mouth. It is believed by some authorities that the hookworm eggs and tiny larvae can actually be scuffed up as dust and be inhaled.

The larva, once in the dog's body, behaves much as the roundworm larva: gets caught in the lungs, passes from blood side to air side of them, passes up the trachea, is coughed up and swallowed in phlegm, and becomes an intestinal parasite. If the afflicted animal be a pregnant bitch, the larvae enter the placenta, as has been described.

One hookworm can suck about half a teaspoonful of blood in a week, so one would not be very serious, but when an animal is infested by thousands, just imagine how much blood the stricken creature must produce in order to live.

Treatment is the same as for roundworms. If there is the least suspicion of hookworm in a kennel, deworm the puppies at three weeks of age. When cured, supply the puppies with food containing iron, such as scraped meat or some baby-puppy food, as early as you can possibly get them to take it.

It is very interesting to realize that bitches caring for pups must themselves consume thousands upon thousands of parasite eggs. This goes on often enough in kennels, and yet fecal examinations often fail to show any parasites in the mother after she has weaned her litter. It may well be wondered why the bitches do not become infested. The reason is that both the roundworm and the hookworm egg require at least a week after they have passed out of the puppy before they can infest another animal.

Tapeworms

There are two common types of tapeworm, and many other rare kinds. Here we shall consider only the two important ones: the flea-host tapeworm and the rabbit-host tapeworm. It is extremely rare to find any other form of tapeworm in the Cocker Spaniel.

The flea-host type is made up of a great many flat segments about half an inch long on the average and about as large as a kernel of rice. The rabbit-host tapeworm is a larger, coarser worm with considerably larger segments. The flea-host tapeworm reaches a length of about 18 inches, while the rabbit-host type may be two feet long.

The symptoms produced by tapeworms are often nervousness, loss of weight, and loss of appetite. The old idea that tapeworms in human beings and dogs cause voracious appetite has not been confirmed by studies. It more often works the other way around, and it always does in dogs, unless they have only one worm, in which case you may notice no difference. But I have known as few as five tapeworms to make a Cocker highly nervous and twitchy, due to the toxins they secreted. A heavy infestation may even affect the coat, which will appear ragged and moth-eaten. The worms, therefore, should be eliminated as soon as possible.

It is easy to detect tapeworms if one watches the stools for about a week, because at least once during the week you will see some of the flattish segments, which may still have the power of movement after they have passed out with the stool. Your veterinarian can detect the presence of the rabbit-host tapeworm by a fecal examination, because large numbers of eggs are laid. The eggs of a flea-host tapeworm are very seldom found in a fecal examination, because the worms hold on to them quite firmly, retaining them in the segments of which they are composed. If one of these segments is squeezed a little, the worm eggs pop out; they look like little clusters of grapes. Very rarely does one find a single egg there: they are almost always in groups, bound together by a filamentous envelope.

The flea-host tapeworm is far more common in Cockers than the rabbit-host tapeworm, because the dogs seldom catch rabbits and eat them. Sometimes a Cocker finds a dead rabbit in the woods, and in that way becomes infested.

The flea-host tapeworm is contracted by the dog from fleas, which, while in the larval stage, have been feeding on the proglottid of tapeworms and eating the tapeworm eggs. These form cysts inside the tiny flea worm which, when it becomes a flea, still has them in its body. It then jumps into the dog's mouth some time when the dog is biting its own skin, and the dog swallows it. One flea has been found to have twenty-five tapeworm cysts in its body, which means that it is theoretically possible for that flea, once digested by the dog's stomach and intestinal fluid, to infest the dog with twenty-five tapeworms. The cysts are actually only the heads of the worms. They attach themselves to the dog's intestine, and from the heads a segment grows, then another, and another, and so on until the worm has reached its full length. Each worm is both male and female, so it does not need more than one to produce fertilized eggs. They are retained, as I said, in the proglottid, and the last proglottid on the worm's body is shed constantly and passed out in the stool, where they make food for flea larvae, and the cycle goes on.

The rabbit-host tapeworm is contracted by the dog eating rabbits which have in turn eaten the eggs of tapeworms, the eggs having stuck to foliage after a dog has defecated on it. Some rabbits have hundreds of cysts in their livers. If you are a hunter and train your dog to run rabbits, be sure you do not feed it rabbit liver, as many Beagle breeders have been known to do, to reward your dog for his efforts. If you do, he is almost certain to become infested with rabbit-host tapeworms.

The removal of tapeworms is very easy if you go about it properly. Some dogs are very easily nauseated by tapeworm drugs. In that case it is best to use arecolene hydrobromide and split the dose. You can buy this in any drugstore, or get it from your veterinarian. The dose is one eighth of a grain to 15 or 16 pounds. Many drug firms put out arecolene in various sizes, but almost all produce one-eighth-grain doses, so that you can give one and a half to the average Cocker and worm him effectively. The dog should be starved for about 18 hours before the drug is administered, and you will find that he will pass the worms within half or three quarters of an hour. If your dog is easily nauseated, break the dose into three parts, giving him one every seven to ten minutes. The drug is cumulative, and will work just as well as if it had been given all at once, and the dog will not be nauseated.

There are many other tapeworm drugs on the market, and they may be had from veterinarians. I know of no other which

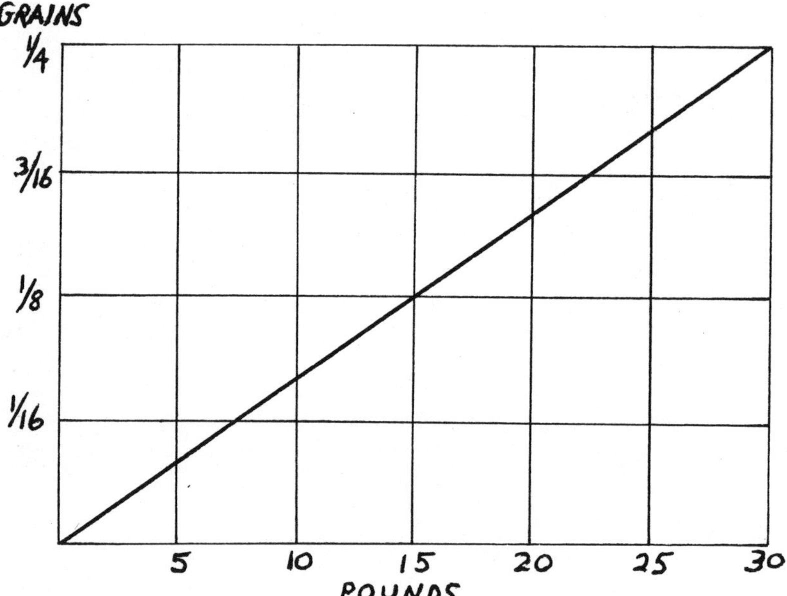

Safe doses of arecolene hydrobromide for robust, empty Cockers.

is obtainable at drugstores. Nemural is a standard, as is Teneathane, and there are others which are newer. But these are the most effective and are recommended.

COCCIDIOSIS

There is hardly a Cocker alive today that has not been affected by some form of coccidiosis. There are three principal forms, one of which involves tiny eggs, another medium-sized eggs, and the third quite large eggs. The first is the revolta form, the second the begimina, and the one with the largest eggs is the felis form, commonly found in cats as well as dogs. They are microscopic entities, and the form of this little protozoan parasite seen in the fecal examinations is actually only the egg form. It changes its shape, and at one time becomes a sort of boring parasite, penetrating the intestinal lining. It is because so many of these parasites—thousands of them—attack the lining simultaneously that there is so much diarrhea and the symptoms of what many people think of as distemper, even including a rise in temperature. If the disease is rampant when puppies are teething, the teeth will often be pitted.

One sees very little coccidiosis in winter: it is mostly a summer disease, and is definitely spread by flies as much as in any other way. It takes only one or two of the parasites to get the disease started in a kennel. Any dog that has once had the disease is a carrier all the rest of its life, so it is almost impossible to find a kennel which is free of it. Personally, I am always very happy once my puppies have had the disease and are over it, because I know they will never have it again. Sometimes I have found all three forms in a dog simultaneously.

When mature dogs contract the disease, it is usually only mildly. Only puppies suffer coccidiosis severely, and sometimes die of it.

After the egg form is ingested, it soon turns into a different form and bores into the intestine lining, where it lives and multiplies. The parasites leave the intestine, create new egg forms, which are passed out in the stool and are the infective forms. Having one infection on top of another is what makes it so difficult for puppies to survive. If a puppy has a single attack and survives it, it becomes immune for life. But if a lot more eggs enter the puppy's intestines, to go through another cycle before the first attack is completed, the enormity of the infection renders the disease very dangerous.

No treatment is known. There are drugs on the market which are excellent when used for chickens and other bird species, but they are useless for dogs. Someday someone will discover something. Many "cures" have been put forward already, but they have not stood the test of careful investigation. One thing is definitely known, and that is that a vitamin-A deficiency renders the dog almost unable to cope with coccidiosis. If a reasonable amount of fat is fed in the diet, along with vitamin A, he should come through the disease with no ill effects.

It is most unfortunate that bitches infect their own puppies with coccidiosis almost always, so that you can count on every litter being affected at some time. This often makes it difficult to sell puppies, because the prospective buyers complain that the puppies have diarrhea.

Coccidiosis is known to veterinarians as "the pet-shop disease," because if puppies go into a pet shop they almost invariably become infected. In our experience as veterinarians we have known literally thousands of puppies to be infected while their owners had no idea what the trouble was. We could only assure them that they must be patient, and that if they would feed fat and a little percomorph oil, say two or three drops a day, in the diet, the puppy would probably recover in a week or ten days.

TRICHINOSIS

It may come as a shock to some Cocker breeders to realize that their dogs can have trichinosis just the same as human beings can, but we have seen not a little of this in Cockers, particularly when they have been house dogs fed on home diets. Trichinosis is nearly always a result of eating undercooked pork. Someone inadvertently feeds the dog some undercooked pork trimmings or meat, and the animal becomes stiff, and it hurts him to walk. We have seen this enough times to know that the trouble is serious, and to warn that no dog should ever be fed raw or undercooked pork, any more than a human being should.

Chapter 13

YOUR COCKER'S HEALTH—DISEASES

Virus Diseases in Dogs

Viruses are tiny infective agents, much like bacteria but considerably smaller—so small, in fact, that many of them will penetrate a porcelain filter along with water. This is something which bacteria cannot do.

THE DISTEMPER COMPLEX

Not many years ago, whenever a dog sniffled and felt sick, he was said to have distemper. Actually the term *distemper* is an old word, applied to human beings first and then to animals, which meant nothing more than "ailment." Today, students have unscrambled the distemper complex, and they know well that it consists of several diseases, each having some individual trait which permits the ailment to be identified and classified.

Carré's Disease

The Frenchman Carré was the first man to show us that the chief disease of what was then called distemper was actually an individual entity and was caused by a virus. This disease is known as Carré's disease, not distemper. Some people still call it distemper, but this is to be deplored because this term is general, not specific.

Today the incidence of the disease has been greatly diminished in some parts of the world, though it is still a menace in others. Symptoms are loss of appetite, nausea, and photophobia (shunning of light). Dogs will act as though the light really hurt their eyes and made them smart. There may also be running fits. The dog's temperature will be 101° for three or four days after the first infection. On the fifth day it may rise to about 104°, and on the sixth drop to normal. On the seventh day it rises once more to 104° or so, and remains high. After the second rise in temperature, the evacuations will be bloody and black; they will have a characteristic odor so obnoxious that those who have seen only a few cases will probably never forget it. It may even pervade a whole house where there is a sick dog. The eyes may be glued together with mucus and are always crusted with a discharge. The nose runs copiously with mucus, which the dog spreads when it sneezes. Sometimes the eyeballs are white with the pus that develops under the lids. After a while, sometimes within two weeks of the start of the disease, the dog may have convulsions. But generally, if the dog develops convulsions or any other symptoms of encephalitis, which is inflammation of the brain, he will not show them for five or six weeks—just about the time one may think the disease is practically over.

An interesting fact about Carré's disease is that a bitch carrying puppies (particularly in the early stages) and becoming infected by the disease simply resorbs the puppies and shows practically no symptoms of the disease. This does not occur in any other canine disease with which I am acquainted.

One of the distinguishing features of Carré's disease is a cough which generally starts about the seventh or eighth day after infection and persists as a dry, hacking cough with very little mucus. It is quite diagnostic, but it must not be confused with coughs caused by many other ailments, such as parasites, for example.

The dog's coat may become rough and unkempt, more or less standing on end, and in some cases one finds pimples on the skin of the belly. The dog becomes dehydrated, and the tongue is sometimes even coated and ulcerated.

Your veterinarian can explain to you about inclusion bodies which are caused by the virus of Carré. They are quite different from the inclusion bodies caused by other diseases, such as rabies, for example.

Carré's disease would sometimes leave dogs blind and deaf if it did not affect the brain. Hunters used to complain that their dogs were worthless after they had once been sick with what their owners then called distemper. The dread disease would sometimes kill every puppy in a litter. Even in grown dogs, depending on the breed, it would take most of them. At one time I had ninety dogs, mostly young, afflicted with the disease, and lost seventy-five of them. Today, however, we would not lose so many because we have antibiotics with which we can at least treat the secondary diseases.

People often ask how long the virus will survive outside the dog. We know that it lives in worms and insects, but not for very many days. The virus itself is quite fragile, and in warm weather will die within 24 hours unless it is protected in some substance like stool, where it may live a little longer. They used to advise burning down the doghouse and practically the entire kennel if "distemper" visited the premises. Today we know that this is entirely unnecessary.

Methods of Protection. There are at least a dozen ways in which dogs can be immunized against Carré's disease. To name a few, there is first the method of Laidlaw and Duncan, which involves the use of a dose of fresh vaccine followed by a dose of live virus. The vaccine establishes temporary immunity, and the virus, while the dog is still filled with antibodies, then produces lifelong immunity. American veterinarians have changed this somewhat, so that two doses of vaccine are given, followed by a dose of live virus. Until very recently it was almost impossible to obtain any live virus, so that the vaccine did whatever good was done, and the third dose was useless. I am strongly opposed to this method, unless one is sure that the virus is alive, and unless one is sure that the vaccine used is very fresh and has been well protected.

Then there is the use of avianized virus. The Lederle Laboratories have developed a method of immunization which, in our hands at least, has proved to be the most effective method yet devised. It involves a single dose of a live virus, which has been attenuated, or weakened, to such an extent that when the dog has the resulting disease the owner does not even know it, but if temperatures are taken, one should note a slight rise about the fifth day. The virus has been passed through ferrets, which attenuated it somewhat, and then has been grown on eggs for as much as fifty passages from one egg to another. There it lives, but changes its form sufficiently for the dog to have only a very mild version of the disease when it is given.

I vaccinate my own pups at four or five weeks of age with half of the usual dose for Cocker puppies. When they are five months old, I give them a full dose, and I have yet to see one puppy develop either Carré's disease or hardpad disease, which we will discuss next.

Some veterinarians prefer to give what they call puppy shots, which are simply doses of serum to protect the dogs against Carré's disease, but if that disease is not in the kennel, the shots are rather useless, expensive, and generally unjustifiable. It is much better to give the live virus when the puppy is still susceptible. When serum is given, the puppy's blood is filled with antibodies from another dog, and they last for quite some time. If the live virus is given, some of the antibodies neutralize it to some extent and make it less effective—at least that is the theory, and that is the way it has worked out in practice. The failures we have seen in the use of live virus are all cases in which serum has either accompanied or preceded the avianized virus.

The Fromm Laboratories have worked out a most excellent method which is effective, as far as all research shows, against Carré's disease. It also consists of the use of a virus attenuated by passage through several ferret passages. The dog is then infected very lightly, and becomes immune to the disease.

There are many variations of the method, and your veterinarian may prefer any one of them to the three I have outlined.

Hardpad Disease

Some say this is a modification of Carré's disease; its symptoms, however, are so entirely different that in my opinion we can consider it a different disease entirely.

It comes at any season, and the dog's temperature is 103° or 104°. But the appetite does not disappear, though it may be poor. The eyes and nose do crust, but there are no long strings of mucus from the nose, and there is no photophobia. The stools remain fairly normal, and there is no obnoxious stench.

The disease drags on, the foot pads becoming hard and linoleumlike. They tend to flatten, and peel off in the later stages if recovery ensues. If the virus reaches the brain, the dog develops encephalitis, with resultant convulsions or twitches, or both.

The only method of immunization which we have found to be effective and sure has been the use of Lederle's avianized vaccine. The old Laidlaw-Duncan methods do not render many dogs immune, but the Lederle's avianized vaccine has been almost 100 per cent successful when enough was given, and when no serum was administered before or with the virus.

House-dog Disease

This is also called laryngo-pharyngo-tracheitis by some investigators. It, too, is caused by a virus, but it is an entirely different disease from both Carré's and hardpad. In the section where I lived it ran wild from about 1940 until 1945 and 1947, and then it practically disappeared. Cases now are very few compared with a few years ago. Certain areas, like St. Louis, Missouri, were badly affected, and so was New England, and in general it tends toward the colder areas and, like the colds of human beings, is a cold weather disease. The saving grace of the disease is that it attacks mostly young dogs, and that a large percentage of those which have it become immune. So many dogs become immune, in fact, that the disease is being wiped out.

The owner first recognizes the disease by noticing that his dog acts as though he has a bone or hair stuck in the throat. In fact, most people present the dog for treatment by saying, "Doctor, my dog has a bone stuck in his throat." On examining the throat, one sees only enlarged tonsils or a reddened throat, which persist for ten days to two weeks, the throat then becoming normal again. The temperature is only about 102.6°. After the dog is cured, he may be immune for life. However, in the case of puppies under six months, about 36 per cent develop encephalitis, leading to convulsions and death, or leaving them with twitches in some parts of the body. The dog sometimes outgrows these twitches, so that after months or years he becomes normal. These things are the worst features of the disease, but the older a dog is the less likely he is to develop encephalitis. Among dogs more than a year old the incidence is only 9 per cent.

As yet we have no means of immunizing against the disease, and certainly dogs immunized against Carré's and hardpad are not immune to house-dog disease. Let us hope that you never experience a siege of it in your kennels.

Infectious Canine Hepatitis

This disease probably has existed for many years, but was called distemper when it did occur. It is now recognized as a separate entity with its own distinct symptoms. In my own experience hepatitis is only serious when young puppies are afflicted. I have seen many mature dogs affected, but none was ill for more than three days, and the symptoms were quite mild.

One reads a great deal about the disease now, however. In fact the serum used against Carré's disease nearly always carries immune bodies against hepatitis, and there is little serum on the market that is not made for both, which shows pretty well how important many people think the disease is.

The symptoms are as follows. The dog generally loses interest in eating, wants to be by himself, and has a temperature of 104° to 105°, which lasts from three to five days. Following this, he usually improves quite rapidly. Sometimes the visible mucous membrane, such as the gums and even the whites of the eyes, may become yellowed with jaundice. There is often a gagging, moist cough, producing phlegm and enlarged tonsils. The stools may be bloody and of a sort of raspberry-jam consistency, although this is not found very frequently. Convalescence is a matter of considerable time, and it will be several weeks before the dogs acts completely normal again.

It must be remembered that the liver has been severely affected by the disease, and because of this the dog could not digest properly, and lost its appetite. The liver, however, repairs itself, and once the repair is complete the dog is normal again.

When a dog becomes sick with hepatitis, I have found that it responds better to glucose than anything else. Even serum does not have a comparable effect. You can either get some dextrose from the drugstore and dissolve it in water, making it just thick enough to pour easily, or you can use Karo syrup and thin it down so it will pour. If a dog the size of a Cocker be given six or eight tablespoons a day, it will feel immeasurably better. But it is not a cure, and only the dog's own body will build up the antibodies necessary for recovery.

The worst effects, as I have said, are in puppies, but the symptoms are different from those in the grown dog. Usually puppies will be all right in the evening and be found dead the following morning. Sometimes death comes so quickly that there are no effects to be seen in a post-mortem examination. If the puppy survives a few days, however, it generally recovers. But if it does die, a veterinarian can diagnose the disease by a thickening of the gall bladder walls, which is a most consistent phenomenon. He will also find pinkish fluid in the abdomen—another fairly accurate criterion. A careful examination of the liver cells will also show inclusion bodies, but this takes a special staining process that most veterinarians are not equipped to carry out. Nor is it generally worth while, for the other pathology speaks for itself.

Rabies

While it is true that throughout the United States thousands of rabies cases have been reported, not all of these occurred in dogs. In places where dogs are kept in kennels and thus off the streets there is almost no rabies to be found.

Symptoms: If your dog should develop a change in personality, if he should start to eat peculiar objects and apparently have lost his sense of taste, tries to drink water but appears to have a paralyzed throat, then look out, because he might have rabies. Take him to a veterinarian at once, handle him as little as possible, and if you have any cuts make certain that if any of the dog's saliva gets on them it is promptly and thoroughly washed out of them. If the veterinarian suspects rabies, he will probably either isolate the dog or destroy him and send the brain to the state laboratory, where tests can be made to determine definitely whether or not the disease is rabies. If it is rabies, serum or the Pasteur treatment should be given to every member of the family who has had any contact with the dog, for rabies is a horrible disease for any human being to die from.

About 50 per cent of dogs are susceptible to rabies, and since yours might be one of them, take every precaution against the disease in the event of exposure. If there is rabies in your state or neighborhood, by all means have your dog vaccinated against it by a veterinarian.

BACTERIAL DISEASES

Leptospirosis

Since it has been found that half the mature dogs in the United States have had leptospirosis without their owners' knowledge, it goes without saying that the disease is a very common one. Some dogs die from it, but most recover. It used to be thought that the disease was caught only from rats, but now we know that it is transmitted by other dogs, chiefly from their urine. Short-legged and long-haired dogs are probably the most susceptible. Leptospirosis is most prevalent among Scottish Terriers, with Cockers running a close second.

The cause of the disease is a spirochete bacterium, which probably enters through the mouth and through the reproductive organs. If an infected dog urinates in a puddle of water, and another dog walks through it or drinks some of it, the chances are excellent that the disease will be transmitted.

Symptoms are loss of appetite and debility. There is elevation of temperature, but high temperature is a fallible indication of the disease. The dog generally becomes quite stiff, and the tiny blood vessels in the whites of the eyes may become enlarged and of a coppery-red color. The liver is affected, and so are the kidneys by the immense number of spirochetes which invade both organs, and the blood also carries them, so the dog naturally has no desire to eat. The stools may be liquid and will sometimes contain blood. The urine is nearly always orange colored; and occasionally chocolate, in which event the dog very seldom recovers.

In some European nations, when a human being goes to a hospital with some of the symptoms of influenza, a test is immediately made for leptospirosis, and the neighborhood from which the patient came is scoured if he has the disease, to find what dog transmitted it to the human being.

There is a new method of immunization which Lederle Laboratories have recently developed, and which I personally believe to be worth-while, even though most dogs do generally recover without any ill effects. However, since nearly everyone fails to use it, most people want to know how to treat their dog once it develops symptoms. Usually when the symptoms are severe enough to attract the owner's attention, the disease has reached a stage just prior to the dog's recovery, and no matter what is done for it, the drug will get the credit. But we do know that the antibiotic drugs known as tetracyclenes are all specific in destroying the spirochetes, and if they are given early enough will greatly relieve the severe part of the disease. These drugs are useful in kennels where one dog develops the disease and others are suspected of having it. Then the disease can be treated effectively; in fact, much more so than in extreme cases in individual dogs.

Pneumonia

At any time of the year a dog may develop pneumonia. The germs are with us and our dogs at all times, and only when the body defenses are lost for some reason, usually unknown, do the germs take over and cause the classical disease. Symptoms: The temperature is around 105°, or even higher. Rasping breath can be heard distinctly with a stethoscope, or, if one puts one's ear against the side of a dog, roaring and gurgling are distinctly audible. The dog loses his appetite and interest in everything, his respirations are very rapid, and he wants to remain quiet. Even the expression on his face seems to indicate that there is something drastically wrong.

Treatment: Dogs seldom die of pneumonia, because, even in the later stages, they can now be placed in an oxygen tent and given antibiotics which produce dramatic cures in most instances. This is a job for your veterinarian, naturally, and he will take care of any case of pneumonia with better than 80 per cent chance of success.

Tonsillitis

This is sometimes caused by viruses, and as we have seen in the cases of house-dog disease and hepatitis, the gagging which indicates something wrong with the throat is a quite constant symptom. However, in the bacterial forms of tonsillitis there is nearly always a very high temperature, around 105° or more. The dog shows great lassitude, some thirst, refuses to eat—not only because of the high fever, but also because it hurts his throat. The tonsils will protrude from the clefts in the throat, often almost as large as small roosters' combs. They are flat and wide, and scarlet in color. The whole throat is often highly pigmented with red, due to the inflammation.

Treatment: Use of antibiotics is the most approved method at present, and the results are excellent, most dogs being cured within three or four days after treatment is begun. But if in one day the dog appears to be so much improved that you can cease the treatment, do not do so, but continue with it for as long as your veterinarian suggests. Relapses often occur, and sometimes they are more serious than the original disease.

DIARRHEA

In young puppies particularly diarrhea is a most serious disease, and can be caused by a wide variety of organisms. It is not so fatal as some diseases, but it can retard a puppy's growth greatly.

In one careful study the ordinary food-poisoning bacterium, that is the salmonella, was found in a large proportion of the dogs studied, and yet these dogs had fairly normal stools.

Treatment: Diarrhea can be handled quite effectively in a number of ways. One of the best is by antibiotics, and even though they are absorbed by the body, they manage to get into the intestinal blood supply so that they soon reduce the intestinal bacteria. There are other drugs that your veterinarian will give you, notably pectin and kaolin, which are often used in combination along with antibiotics.

We have already mentioned the way in which coccidiosis affects dogs, causing diarrhea. If this is the case with your dog, do not expect the diarrhea to be cured by any drugs that are given. It will be cured only when the dog itself builds up immune bodies.

These have all been diseases of a general nature which occur in Cockers. From here on we can mention some of the more common Cocker ailments of a more specific kind.

SKIN DISEASES

We have already discussed red mange and sarcoptic mange, and have indicated how to treat them. There is another whole class of skin infections which occur in the damp, warm parts of the year. Some of these are undoubtedly started by fleas, so by keeping your dog well covered with flea powder you can greatly diminish the chance of any of these diseases becoming established. When a dog is badly infested, it nibbles at itself to kill the fleas, and thereby keeps the area moist. In this moisture and warmth fungus spores and some bacteria develop around the skin, some in the hair follicles and some in the glands.

Skin specialists recognize at least a dozen different diseases, such as acne, eczema, etc., etc. Here we will group them together, because they are generally so easily cured by any one of several outstanding and rather new skin remedies. At the Whitney Veterinary Clinic skin diseases never presented any particular problems to us, because we thought that our remedy, which we had developed over many years, was the most effective ever found. Then along came a new antibiotic called Malucidin. This, to my knowledge, is the first antibiotic which is also a fungicide and is not poisonous to an animal. It is made from spent brewers' yeast by a patented process, and is the most remarkable remedy we have ever tried for any of the common forms of dog skin disease. Most veterinarians can supply you with it in four- or eight-ounce bottles, or larger sizes.

If itching appears on the dog, it is well to dose him liberally with Malucidin, and even the big, wet, so-called hot spots which used to be called moist eczema will sometimes be cured by two applications. The preparation has a small amount of liquid soap in it, which helps it to spread quickly over the skin, so that a small quantity covers a large area, therefore it is inexpensive on that account.

When a dog is covered from head to foot with a skin disease, sometimes another recent discovery, solenium sulphate, may be applied in a soap base. This will have to be done at your veterinarian's, for it is a poisonous substance, and users are warned that it cannot be left on the dog for more than five minutes, or it may become toxic to him. The dog is given a bath, using the remedy as a kind of soap, and it is left on him for five minutes before being removed. It has proved very effective especially in cases where large areas have been diseased.

Dogs that have fleas will often suffer from their mouth moisture causing a new area to become infected. So it is wise to use a flea powder in which is incorporated a fungicide. There are several of these on the market, and all of them stem from a discovery which I made and published in *Veterinary Medicine Magazine* several years ago. Most of those on the market use a fungicide called spurgon. You can obtain this from the Naugatuck Chemical Company, but it seems much cheaper to buy the flea powder already mixed. If a powder with rotenone for the flea-killing agent and spurgon for the fungicide is used, one has a double-barreled remedy which should keep a dog free from skin diseases throughout the summer.

ANAL GLAND AILMENTS

Just under the anus and on each side of it there is a small gland equivalent to that which the skunk possesses. It is also very common in many other species of animal. These glands have very little use so far as we can tell. When you see a dog dragging his hindquarters along the ground, he is trying to squeeze out the contents of the gland. When this happens, one can be sure that there is either an infection or too great an accumulation of the material the gland houses.

Treatment: It is only necessary to cover one's right hand with a piece of cotton and to feel through the skin of the dog to locate the small glands. When they are normal, they will be no larger than a yellow-eye bean, but when filled with fluid they may be as large as small chestnuts. Pressure should be exerted underneath and behind them, and if you squeeze hard and persistently enough, the muscle that holds the contents in place will relax, and they will be forced out through two small ducts at the mouth of the anus. Sometimes this material will be black, tarry, and very hard to squeeze out; normally it is a yellowish color and clear, but occasionally there will be curds and the substance will have the consistency of clay. It always has an obnoxious smell, and the only dog that likes it is the one who possesses it: he will try to clean himself up. It is obnoxious to other dogs, and especially so to human beings who get it on their hands. One's hands should be washed at once, as the odor will remain in the skin for many hours.

Chapter 14

GROOMING YOUR COCKER

The amount of grooming you will have to do depends upon the breed of Cocker you have chosen. If it is American or English, it will be light, and a minimum of equipment is necessary. If you own a Woolly Cocker, you need more, and must spend much more time. If you can afford it, have him groomed by a professional once a month, or at least once in two months. Comb him yourself daily, if possible.

Equipment

A steel comb should be your first implement. There are many makes to be had. A comb with teeth one inch long and twelve teeth to the inch is ideal. But many combs are made with teeth that bend under hard usage or soon drop out. In our professional work we have never found the equal of the Resco F comb for Cocker care. You can obtain one at almost any dog supply store.

A *brush,* too, is a must, and this can be any fairly stiff and inexpensive scrubbing brush, or as expensive a one as you wish. Your Cocker will like a brushing with a stiff brush better than he will one with a soft one.

The kind of Cocker which made the breed so popular and possessing a coat which required a minimum of care.

A *razor-blade dresser* is useful to remove stray hair and keep the coat flat.

Scissors are useful for trimming the foot hair and shortening feather and ear hair.

Electric clipper, with number-2 blade, if it is an Oster. But only those with Woolly Cockers need one. If you have such a dog, unless you intend to have it groomed entirely professionally, add the cost of this instrument to that of the dog, and expect to use it often. The cost in 1955 is about $40.

Toenail clippers and file. The guillotine type of the former is best. Only if you expect to show your dog will a nail file be necessary, and maybe not even then. A house dog running on concrete will file his own nails, unless you fail to keep the hair trimmed under his feet.

Besides these you can buy a wide variety of gadgets—thinning shears, glove brushes, oils, and so on. Get them if you wish, but with the above items an expert can put a Cocker into show shape.

THE ART OF GROOMING

As we have seen, it was the groomer who set the present style of the show Cocker. Perhaps grooming really is the art it is supposed to be, but if so there are a lot of dog-clipping Rembrandts, Corots, and Rodins who learned their dog art in a week or less. I have instructed many who can turn out beautiful Cockers from mops of hair so large that it is hard to find the dog inside them.

Suppose we start with your Woolly Cocker. If your dog has hair growing long on any part of his legs other than the rear, that will place him in the Woolly breed. You have bought a clipper, comb, scissors, and toenail trimmers. Let's go.

If he is inclined to snap, tie a face tie tightly about his mouth with the knot under his chin, and, bringing the ends of your tie along the cheeks, tie them together in a bow knot behind the ears. If the dog won't stand still, move the table under a curtain pole or something to which you can attach a chain, the other end of which you fasten to the dog's collar. We assume this is his first clipping: every dog is suspicious of the buzzing clipper until he learns that it feels good on his skin.

Now, with the dog's head held up in a show pose, start on his rear end and gradually work forward, but clipping from front to back—not "against the grain." If your dog is used to clipping, start at the head and trim it "with the grain" from his nose,

Idahurst Roderic, as wonderful in every respect as was his mother Idahurst Belle II. He lived to be 15 and one of his sons, 16.

continuing right to the tip of the tail. Trim down the sides in accordance with the pattern shown on the opposite page. As you clip the head, leave the hair longish over the brows to accentuate the stop. Trim under the tail as far down as you have on the sides, so the dog has the general appearance of wearing a skirt of long hair.

If the dog is nippy or nervous at the start, by the time you have finished the rest of the body and begin working on the head he will have lost a lot of his fear and apprehension. You may be able to remove the mouth tie and clip the foreface and cheeks which the cloth covered.

Trimming the feet should be a part of every cocker's grooming. The foot in any breed of Cocker should be cat-foot type, roundish that is, and without long hair. This is equally true of the Woolly Cocker, even though his other long leg hair covers the feet. Most groomers snip off or clip the hair about an inch from the ground. The foot bottom should be trimmed carefully, too, and the nails clipped just short enough so that when the dog's weight is on the foot, the nails do not quite touch the table top on which he is standing.

The English and American Cockers need very little grooming. Let us hope the day will soon dawn when these two breeds may be shown entirely naturally, except for combing and brushing. That would definitely do more than anything else to return the American breed to top popularity.

Today, with these two breeds as they are, if you own a black-and-white particolor the black spots almost always have much longer hair than the white, so your razor-blade dresser can be used to shorten this hair and smooth the coat.

Combing is not difficult, nor do you have to comb often, except in cases where the dog may have some straw or burrs in the ears. If he develops some lumpy snarls, a little mineral oil poured into them will enable you to unsnarl the dog easily, but after that he needs a bath to wash out the oil.

The nails need trimming at times, and the dewclaws should always be suspect, because they do not reach the ground to wear off. If they have grown into the foot, have your veterinarian cut them. If you trim a nail and it bleeds, put the dog somewhere where the blood can't harm the surface. The bleeding will soon stop. The next day it is best to keep the dog off hard surfaces, or he may wear the nail sufficiently to make it bleed again. Many nails grow so long that if they are to be pruned to the proper length they will have to bleed. Nor can you shorten them a little today and more next week: you must do it and get it over with, and thereafter keep the nails the right length by frequent trimming, or by walking your Cocker on hard pavement.

Shedding

An outdoor dog who has no access to artificial light has a good shedding once a year, and that is all. A dog kept under artificial light part of every day may shed a little all the year round. Why?

Evidence points to the fact that the cycle produced by the changing length of the day is responsible for shedding. The coat comes out as soon as the days have lengthened materially, and is completed by August or earlier. The new coat grows, and by September has reached its prime, and is kept until next shedding season.

Remove this cycle's influence from the dog by turning on electric lights when the days are shorter, letting him stay in the home with you and go to sleep when you turn out the lights, and you have provided him with days of uniform length all the year through, except that some get light earlier in the morning and the dog awakens before you do. His shorter days are therefore of considerably longer duration than the outdoor dog's, and his long days are of the same length. No wonder he sheds a little all the year round.

There is no other cure for this other than putting your Cocker in an unlighted room as soon as it is dark outside. Do that and the shedding will be only in early and midsummer. But you won't do that, nor would I, so just comb him frequently and he will not be a nuisance.

Chapter 15

TRAINING YOUR COCKER—BASIC PRINCIPLES

Now I realize, of course, that there are thousands of dog owners who have rationalized the dog up into the realm of the human being. You even read such statements by authors on dog training as, "The dog is not a seal, so don't feed him when you train." Many dog owners, especially those who have helped give Cockers an evil reputation by spoiling their dogs until they had nasty dispositions, will tell you it is cruel to discipline a dog in any way except scolding.

Well, it is true that dogs can be trained without rewards by the system presently in vogue—the force system—and it is true that Cockers can be trained without physical discipline. But just compare the efficiency of the methods and the effect on your dog of those outworn fifteenth-century methods with the new ones based on modern psychology. A dog isn't a seal; he may not be quite so bright as a seal, and he is definitely not of human mental caliber. So treat him and train him for what he is, and your rewards and pleasure from what you will learn yourself will be immeasurably increased.

With the new methods you can train your Cocker in a tenth of the time most persons spend.

BASIC PRINCIPLES FOR TRAINING

We start out with the established fact that *a dog's behavior is never uncaused*. The brain receives impressions from the senses and reacts to them. The pattern of reaction depends in part on the dog's inheritance. As we have observed in Chapter VII, Cockers have inherited, through many generations of selection, certain patterns of behavior. In training, our best results may be obtained by building on this fact.

Every dog has reflexes. He hears a sound, and cocks his ears; he smells food, his mouth waters; he tastes disagreeable food, and spits it out; he touches a hot coal, and jerks his foot away, and so on *ad infinitum*. We can let him be a child of nature and do whatever his reflexes cause him to do, or we can condition his reflexes so that he does what we want him to do. Most dogs are practically untrained because the owners are too ignorant, too indolent—or both—to train them.

This is the way a reflex is conditioned: simultaneously with the stimulus which evokes the action we add another stimulus—a sound, a flash of light, or a sensation. If the two occur enough times together, either part of the combination may be dispensed with and the dog will react in the same uniform way. Salivation was the original reaction on which conditioning was studied, and it makes as good a one as any to use as an illustration. Show a dog food and his mouth waters. Ring a bell at the same time you show him food, and his mouth waters. Repeat many times. Now ring the bell without the food being present, and his mouth will water just the same.

How does this differ from such an action as the following? You are walking around the rough in a golf course. Your Cocker has been taught to retrieve golf balls—an uncommonly

If a puppy is smacked with a broom and each time he hears a word, after two or three repetitions he will run when he hears the word.

easy feat for him. You throw a golf ball into the rough and he retrieves it by sight and by its odor. He learns by the direction you swing your arm where to run. So now you swing your arm but do not throw a ball. Away he tears into the rough and sniffs around for the rubbery odor. He finds a faint odor and gets a golf ball, bringing it to you. With a Cocker equipped with such a conditioned reflex you can earn spending money and get exercise most enjoyably.

Or how does the saliva illustration differ from the case where your dog jumps up against you? This you have inadvertently conditioned him to do previously. But now you decide that it must stop, so you seem to pet him as you have always done, but as you cover his eyes with a hand you also step on a hind foot, hard enough to hurt him. You and every other member of the family step on his foot every time he jumps up, but you try

It pays well to start posing puppies early, even though they may never be shown. This makes them independent and better dogs. The handling is good for them.

not to let your dog know you do it. What have you accomplished? You have simply made him realize that jumping up gives him a pain in a hind foot. So he doesn't jump up.

If you have never thought about it, remember that you must give a meaning to a sound. Words are sounds of no meaning to your Cocker until you have impressed on him what the meaning of each word is. A toot on a whistle, the ringing of a bell, the sound of a hunter's horn, and even the hum of the motor in a certain car are all sounds which can be given meanings. Giving meaning to sounds is a principal part of training.

Ideal training conditions as many reflexes at one time as possible. Actually much more of a dog's brain is involved in the conditioning of most reflexes than was formerly thought. When a dog feels a hot coal, not only does his foot snap away from it, his whole body recoils, and he trots a considerable distance from the pain-producing spot.

Conditioning over and over amounts to habit formation. That you must keep in mind. Results may be achieved by punishments and by rewards. Punishments may be the sort of thing which the dog realizes he brings on himself, such as an electric shock when he barks, or he may have an out-and-out realization that his misdeed causes you to punish him.

Rewards may be accomplishments—the realization that an action brought the desired result—or they may simply be some food you give the dog when he is hungry. Rewards supply your dog with fulfillment of a strong desire. As an example, you take his kennel mates for a walk and leave him behind. He jumps frantically at the gate and strikes the latch. The door opens: he dashes after you. Two or three repetitions of this behavior, and the dog has learned how to open the door. Or he is hungry, and he learns that doing a certain act a certain way brings a reward—food.

To train, we need to establish in our dog a great want—a drive, a stimulus—which we can fulfill with a reward, and to keep on supplying the reward until we have carried our conditioning forward to such an extent that it becomes the established pattern of behavior.

These rewards psychologists call reinforcements. Now what are some of the drives and the rewards which you can use in Cocker training?

Food. Small tidbits to be given only when the dog is *hungry.*

Companionship. Used negatively—making a dog think you are leaving home when he wants to go can have excellent results.

Love of work. Giving your Cocker an opportunity to do what his inherited behavior patterns urge him to do can be an excellent reward. Suppose he loves to hunt rabbits, and at every opportunity will go out into a brush lot and drive rabbits by the hour; simply giving him this privilege can be used as a reward. Letting him retrieve is an excellent illustration. He naturally, by inheritance, loves to carry small objects. He also naturally loves to run after one, but he doesn't know you will throw it until you have shown him. So in a few minutes he will learn that to drop the object at your feet means that you will throw it, and that is all the reward he needs. You need not give him food for returning the object, but if you do, you will reinforce the lesson even more strongly.

Brushing with a stiff brush can act as a reward once a dog has been taught to stand. You can show him the brush and point to a chair or table, and he will bounce on to it. Or you can say a word—chair, table—and he will act the same way after a few lessons.

On the negative side, what means of punishment are available for training? First, the old, simple methods:

The open hand. A sharp slap beside the face is generally an excellent punishment. Don't let anyone convince you that the hand must be used only to reward the dog. The hand, he soon learns, is just, rewarding for right acts, and disciplining for wrong.

The feet. Many experienced dog trainers believe that a dog watches their feet first, so they use them as indicators and as means of punishment. Big-game hunters often ride down miscreant hounds who have run on deer tracks and let the horse trample them. Some dog trainers kick and stamp on their dogs or, as some Midwestern backwoodsmen say, *tromp on 'em,* and whether we approve or not, they have dogs that work for them like demons, and behave ideally.

The rolled newspaper. This makes a crackling noise when the dog is struck with it. The trouble is that most amateur dog trainers do not strike hard enough.

Shaking. There are few more satisfactory means of punishment than picking the misbehaving dog up by the neck and just shaking him until you think his teeth will drop out. A mild shake at first, of course, but violent if the mild one has proved ineffective.

The switch. A proper switching must really hurt the dog. Don't "cut the tail off an inch at a time" by a lot of annoying little taps, but pick the miscreant up by the back of the neck and wallop him along the side.

The broom. There is no more natural means of punishment in the hands of a woman than a broom. A good swish is excellent punishment for a puppy, and for a really obstreperous dog, a well-worn broom makes a wonderful tool. But it must never be used to chase a dog with. The dog must be tied where he can't crawl into a doghouse or under a bed. A barking dog can be chained to a radiator, for instance, and when he barks, the words *be quiet* can be said accompanied by a wallop with the broom. After a while you can discontinue using the broom and *be quiet* is all you need say.

The dark closet. Most dogs, and Cockers especially, dread being alone and confined in the dark. For punishment, simply bundling the dog ignominiously into a dark closet for an hour can be used to excellent effect.

Water. Squirting water on an outdoor Cocker, throwing a half bucket of cold water over him, and filling the bucket and leaving it where he can see it ready for the next lesson works well. So does placing a half barrel of water next to his kennel and, when he barks, rushing out, making him realize he is calling you, and picking him up and pushing him under the water. But water is a warm-weather punishment, of course.

Blackstone's Reflector, with long legs, built for speed and an excellent hunting type.

The electric shocker. For many years now—more than thirty—I have occasionally used a device I made which beats every other method of negative training. It is based on a dog's dislike of the tiniest electric shock. An amount of electricity which to us is almost pleasant will make a dog recoil with a jolt. And if such punishment is properly used there is no better method. I like it because it makes the dog realize that his action gives him a shock. Anyone can make such a device, but only a serious trainer or breeder is likely to do so. It consists of a dry cell, a small induction coil, a dog collar with pointed studs (two on each side, with two insulated), and a pair of wires running from the studs to the coil. There is a switch, of course. The collar is placed on the dog and the double wire acts as a leash. To give you one example of its use if the dog chews on his leash a touch of the switch gives him a shock and one or two shocks will stop such an action.

There are a few specifications of punishments which must be kept in mind:

It should hurt or frighten. This is nature's way. Watch dogs disciplining one another, or a bitch teaching her pups, and you realize that anything you or I are likely to do will be mild by comparison.

It must make your dog know that you are his boss and master, and no fooling.

You must not undertake any training on even a small problem unless you are prepared to follow through to final conditioning.

In positive conditioning there should be no punishment until your dog is performing the act correctly at least 75 per cent of the time. That is the punishment must be for the dog failing to do something he has learned and knows how to do.

Punishment must be immediate, if possible as part of the wrong act of the dog, like the burn from the hot coal, or the electric shock or mouth burn when a puppy chews an electric cord. A dog's attention may be on something entirely different, if punishment is postponed, and you will give him the feeling he is being punished for that instead of the act for which you are really chastising him. A good illustration of such stupid training is when a dog owner returns home and finds a dog has evacuated indoors and he sticks the dog's nose in the stool and scolds. I doubt that any dog that ever lived was housebroken by that method.

Chapter 16

TRAINING THE HOUSE DOG

Because a Cocker is first and rightly a hunting dog, you may say we should take up the matter of hunting first. But actually so few Cockers ever get a chance to hunt that hunting is an aspect of Cocker usage which interests only a handful of persons. For that we should be sorry, because every Cocker owner could have much more fun from ownership if he did train and use his little dog in this interesting way. Actually there were only 33 Cocker field trials held under A.K.C. auspices during 1954: the number should have been a thousand or more. But since "that's the way it is," we shall deal with Cockers as house dogs first.

Behavior-training classes have become exceedingly popular, but not nearly so popular as they should be. Behavior training is basically the training of a dog to be a good companion. But it goes much further than that, because those who are bitten by this benign bug become filled with enthusiasm and the spirit of competition, and show no desire to quit. Soon they are exhibiting their dogs for prizes, and many people go on from one class to another, often aiding the newcomers to learn the lessons they have already learned themselves.

Almost all of the trainers were taught in the old or force system: that is, you push your dog's rear end down and say *sit* until he has learned to do it to order. Contrast this system's results with those of the reward system of getting the dog to sit of his own volition and then rewarding him! Surely the latter is ten times as efficient.

Postitive Training

Let us take a few simple positive acts we wish our Cocker to perform. What shall our incentive or drive be? Hunger. That is painless and, apparently, magic. So we shall see our Cocker has only water to drink for 36 hours. He will then be hungry enough really to *try*. (He will not be harmed—a dog has lived for 117 days on water without food.)

We are going to teach him:

1. To get on the *table*. This is a useful command for him to execute, because an old table makes an excellent place on which to comb and brush him;
2. *Down* from the table;
3. *Shake hands;*
4. *Other paw;*
5. *Lie down;*
6. *Stand;*
7. *Sit.*

How long would it take by the force method to train him to

execute these seven commands? Try it on your Cockers if you have untrained ones, and compare. By the reward method you will certainly have your dog executing the orders within two evenings if you keep him hungry. Starve him first for 36 hours, after which your reward will be his food. Then give him nothing but water again for 24 hours. Then let him rest a day, and

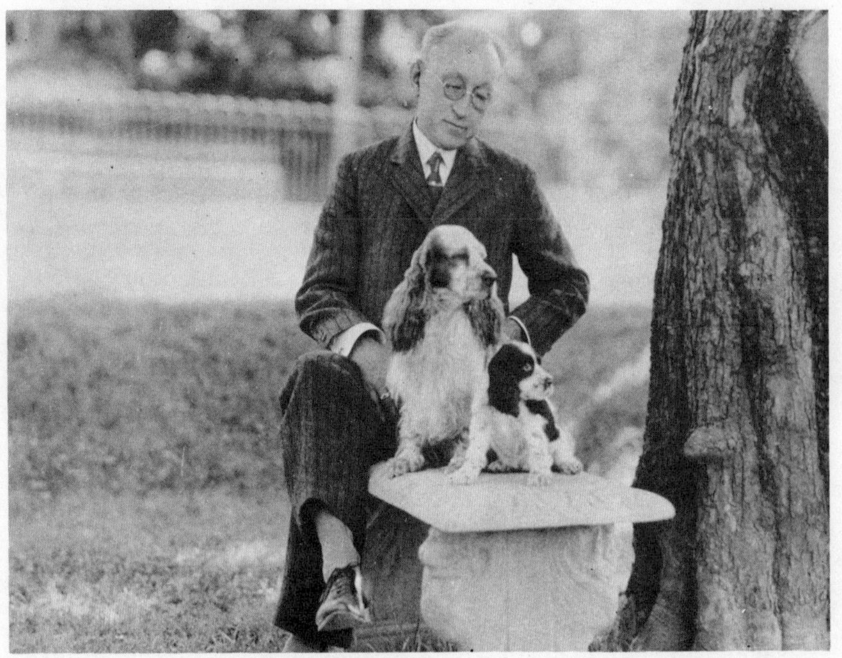

O. B. Gilman, for many years America's largest Cocker breeder.

thereafter feed him only what he barely needs to live on—800 calories a day for a Cocker. He should be hungry enough to eat eagerly a dry crust of bread, and you will choose something more tempting than that. I suggest half-inch lumps of frankfurter or pieces of hamburger as large as a thimble.

You have probably read enough about training, or seen enough of it, to know that nearly all trainers want you to pronounce your dog's name before any command. But this I know is entirely unnecessary unless you are training a lot of dogs performing together and want to call one out from the pack to perform individually. "George—sit" and "George—lie down" and "George—jump" gets tiresome and are needless. Your dog knows you are talking to him.

Get on the *table*. Your key word is *table*. So use only that. Set a chair beside your training table; neither of them must shake or tremble. With Nero—that's your dog's name in this chapter—having sniffed the reward in your hand, you say *table* and let him follow your hand first up on the chair and thence on to the table. He gets his reward and wants more.

Down from the table. Say *down,* and let him follow your hand down. When he is down, he gets his reward.

Pause a minute, get his attention, and say *table,* going through the same routine as many times as it takes for him to get up on the table without a movement of your hand. All this will probably take you 30 minutes at most.

Shake hands. Put a harness or collar on Nero. Put a ring—an eye bolt—in the wall behind the table, which will be tight against the wall. The ring should be about ten inches from the floor. Run a light chain with a swivel in it from the ring in the harness or collar back to the ring in the wall. This chain should be just long enough for Nero's chest to come even with the front edge of the table.

Did you ever see what a hungry dog does when he can't reach food with his mouth? He reaches for it with his paw, doesn't he? Take advantage of that fact. Let Nero smell the meat, and the moment his foot comes forward to reach it, say *shake,* and give him his reward. In a few minutes you'll have him batting at you when you say *shake*. Then it is your time to teach him *other*.

Other paw. When he finds pawing with one foot doesn't get him the food, he will try to reach it with the other foot, which will be accompanied by your word *other*. Feed him only for the correct foot coming forward on the word *other*. He will soon learn that *shake* means the right foot and *other* the left, or, if

Knight's Flashy Flash—one of the few great modern winners with the American Cocker coat.

you prefer, *shake* may mean whichever he presents first and *other* the alternate foot.

After he is proficient at this job on the table, let him get down and try his reactions on the floor.

The second evening can well start with repetition of the previous evening's training before beginning new commands.

Lie down. Tie Nero with a short chain running from his harness or collar to the ring in the wall behind him. Let him shake a few times and then say *lie down,* and hold your reward just below the table top so he must lie down to reach it. When he is down, give it to him.

Stand. At once teach him what *stand* means. I like the word *up* but, as you will see, the word *hup* is used as a field trial command meaning to sit, and the two words sound too much alike for contradictory uses.

You teach *stand* by holding the reward high so that Nero has to stand up to get it.

Sit is taught by holding the reward in your closed hand close to his face and making him back up. He will soon sit, and you say the word as he does so. Repeat until he knows the meaning of the word.

Having taught him this simple execution of your words, or, to put it another way, having conditioned Nero to associate word sounds with actions, you can go on applying the principle to actions off the table.

Repetition over and over again finally evokes immediate response to the words. If he does not respond, he needs more table training. Here are a few useful actions you can elicit by the use of words:

Come. Train your hungry Nero in an enclosure. Let him wander away and say *come* or just whistle. Feed him his little reward and wait for him to wander again. When you and he have repeated the action so many times that he seems to understand the word, try him another day in the open with a long training cord. When he seems to respond without a mistake, get a friend to provide something alluring, to see if the dog will fail to mind you. Walking a strange dog on a leash where Nero can see him is one of the best lures. Hold on to the training cord so the dog completely upsets himself when he comes to its end, and when he is thus discommoded call him and reward him when he comes. Or let a cat out of a bag so he can see it run away. Call *come,* and when he fails to do it, he tumbles in a

Training to retrieve.

heap at the end of the training cord. A few such lessons teach him that you can reach out and control him. You can then make the cord longer and longer.

Please note that you cannot train Nero vicariously: you do it, not just sit in an armchair and think about it.

Fetch or *get* is a useful action to teach, and easier than many know. Since Nero loves to retrieve, just throw anything and he will run to it, pick it up, and carry it. If you start with a hungry Nero, you can use rewards to teach him to discriminate between several objects, say a brush, a slipper, and his leash. Under negative training we shall see how to train a dog to realize what *no* means. In this case you can throw two objects and tell Nero to *get slipper*. If he starts to pick up the brush which you have tossed with the slipper you say *no,* and then

Field Trial Champion Barry of Ware shows how he retrieves. Much training can be carried on in the back yard.

when he picks up the slipper and brings it to you, he gets his reward. Later you can teach him what *brush* means, and *leash,* so you can throw out all three objects and he will retrieve the one you tell him to bring you.

From his differentiating in this way it is only a step to teach him to get your slippers, his brush, or his leash whenever you request them, or to take the evening paper from the paper boy and bring it to you.

I hope that by now you see how easy it is to train. Of course it takes hours of patient repetition as you give word and other sound meanings to Nero, but what could be more worth-while?

Teaching him to walk at your side, which obedience-class trainers call *heeling,* is only a matter of walking with Nero, keeping him on a leash at your left side, and commanding him to *sit* every time you stop. I prefer the words *at side* for this, and to train him that *heel* means what it used to; namely, to walk behind me just as the heel-driving Shepherd dogs "dog the footsteps" of cattle, sheep, of their owners, or Dalmatians heel behind horses. All one needs is a leash and a switch and some rewards to accomplish both objectives.

Negative Training

This general kind of training in what *not* to do is simpler and requires much less thought than positive training, and here is where punishments are used intelligently.

When a dog misbehaves, he is not doing it because he is necessarily innately bad or trying to annoy you: he was inadvertently trained that way by you or someone previously. The barking dog furnishes an excellent example. It is a natural reaction for any dog to bark. He begins very young, and usually nothing is done to stop him. Why wouldn't he bark?

As he grows older he may bark when he is hungry. What does his owner, who is annoyed by the barking, do? Unfortunately he feeds him, and thus reinforces the barking reaction to hunger.

Once a reflex has become conditioned in this way, to uncondition it is to see either that it is not used for several months, or to shock the dog severely with punishment, so that the one reaction overcomes the other. We know this not only from animal psychology, but from human. Most of us have been conditioned in certain ways: to stand when "The Star Spangled Banner" is being played, for example, and if we were to sit when it was played before a ball game we should have a guilty feeling. For months after Hitler died, if someone said "Heil, Hitler" to a German, it was difficult for the hearer not to salute.

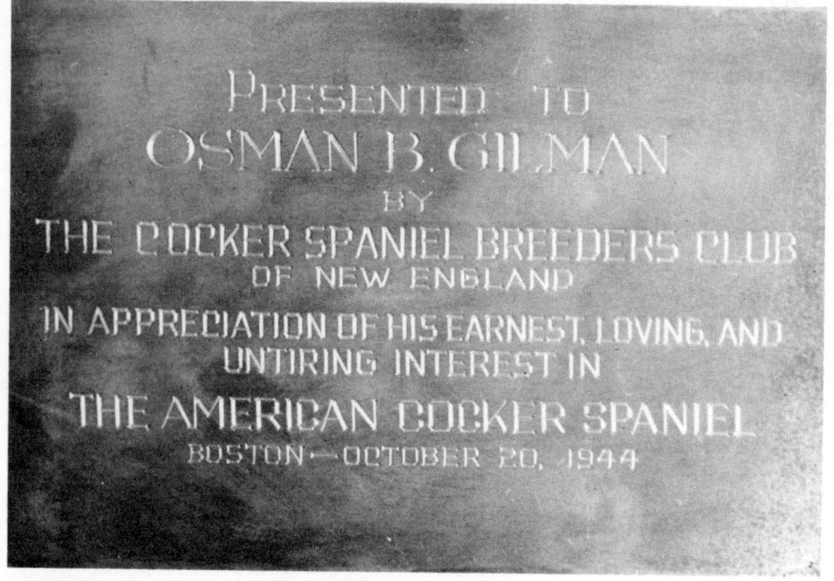

A memorial to loving untiring interest which was so richly deserved.

The less-complicated dog acts simply, positively, and negatively. So, brain washing for him—washing out the previously conditioned reflexes—can best be achieved by punishment. We have seen what some of those methods can be. And now, knowing roughly what the conditions are, one realizes how much sternness, persistency, and patience may be necessary to brainwash, to decondition, and to recondition Nero. Here are a few useful negative commands and how to apply them:

No. I start every dog I ever train by teaching this simply taught expletive. It is easy to say, and the dog learns it as easily as a puppy learns to keep away from his mother's food when she growls—her way of saying *no.* And your punishment need not be so severe as the bitch's, either, to accomplish similar understanding by the puppy or dog.

If you are using your hand to discipline, drop a bone with meat on it before your hungry dog. Be sure the food is too large for him to swallow. Say *no* sharply as he goes to take it, and slap his face. Train him in an empty room where he can't hide away. I would not use an electric shocker here, because it will be ever so much more difficult to get him to take the food when you come to teach that.

As you slap him, he drops the meat. Leave it there, and every time he starts to take it say *no* and slap. In a few minutes he will know the meaning of *no* as it applies to that one object. So now you must train him to know the meaning of the sound *take it,* or *take.* You may actually have to put the meat in his mouth and let him chew on it. Keep dropping rewards and say *take* it over and over, and suddenly intersperse the *take it's* with *no.* If he takes the meat, reach right into his mouth and pull it out, and slap.

When he has learned these commands, try throwing the enticing food a distance of, say, five feet from you and saying *no,* and, once the dog has obeyed, *take it.* Next, stand in the doorway of the room and repeat this. The whole thing should not take you more than an hour to teach Nero. Now you are ready to apply the word *no* to other activities, and if you are firm, never letting an exception occur, you will have done your dog and yourself a great service. You can use the word for anything he should not do—chase cars, bark, hook his chin on to the food or water dish and tip it, and so forth.

Stay. *Staying* in one spot while you, the dog's master, walk away is a negative response. Nero's natural response will be to follow you. Have him lie down, and say *stay* while you back away. If he moves, say *no*. After a few minutes' delay, tell him to come, and reward him. Repeat, lengthening the delay until he will stay as long as you wish. You can accompany your command with a motion if you wish, such as a Hitler salute (this is the usual obedience-class gesture), and, when you drop your hand, call *come*. Soon the dog will watch your hand, and you can dispense with the word. Practice him often, and he will become adept.

Honey Creek Harmonizer—a beautiful animal, with an extra long coat for a parti-colored dog.

Chapter 17

TRAINING THE HUNTING COCKER

A Cocker field trial is an approximation of a bird hunt. There is more certainty, because birds can be planted or the trial may be held in the well-stocked hunting preserve of a Cocker enthusiast. The question at once comes to mind, "Why are not Cocker field trials much more popular?" And it demands an answer.

I cannot give one. While Beagle and Coonhound trials have gone on breaking records, Cocker trials have stood still or have never really caught on. Yet there is in them all the sport of beagling, and of upland bird hunting with the larger type of bird dogs. Mrs. Ella Moffit worked hard to popularize them, as did Elias Vail, Ralph Craig, Clarence Pfaffenberger, and many others. The competitions have not been confined to wealthy persons: they were and are democratic, but have not clicked as they should have. Yet I think they will, and thousands of people will find in the sport something they have sought in vain.

Compared with training Sheepdogs or Coonhounds, Cocker training is one of the simplest tasks, and those who think it is difficult have just never known other breeds and what goes into training them. Beagles are even simpler to train, because all the dog has to do is exhibit his natural bent for following rabbit trails, just as the Cocker exhibits his for bird interest. It remains only to teach the Beagle that he must run only rabbits.

In training for hunting or field trials, the same commands need to be used for both. And a well-trained hunter is also a field trial dog except that he needs to be accustomed to the human element. A Cocker who has been trained to be with only his own master, who shoots the bird when it rises, may be uncomfortable when two or three persons accompany himself and his owner, the others being judges or the gunner, called, in bird-dog parlance, *the gun.*

Just what does bird hunting require of a dog?

First, the love of hunting and interest only in birds.

Second, that he sit, upon order, when he finds the bird and flushes it. This is called steadiness to wing.

Third, steadiness to shot.

Fourth, the ability to watch where the bird falls, and retrieve it, dead or alive, upon command.

Fifth, to carry it gently—with a soft mouth.

Sixth, if the bird is wounded, and runs or hops away and hides, to find it by trailing or air scenting.

Seventh, great endurance.

In training any dog for hunting there are two principal systems in vogue. One is to let the dog run wild after all kinds of birds and animals. This is supposed to develop his hunting instinct, preseverance, and endurance. Then, when he has become a wild, tough hunter, you cut him down to doing only what you want him to do.

The second way is to train him in the separate elements of hunting, and punish him for wrongdoing. These elements are retrieving, sitting on command, flushing and retrieving on command, and steadiness to gun. If each of these separate ingredients of the whole is understood, the dog, if he is a real bird

Any typical American Cocker has jaws large enough to retrieve a grouse, as this retriever so plainly shows.

dog at heart, will be almost broken for hunting from the start, and have no improper conditioning to be unlearned. Old-time hunters may call this a theory, but by this second method a dog may be trained in a fraction of the time.

We start with a powerful drive—the opportunity to do something the dog was bred for. He's made to order for it, and neither food nor sex nor many other drives are so potent.

So we train him in the separate elements of the whole, and at last take him hunting when he knows the meaning of our word sounds.

Hup. We have already mentioned this command. To reinforce it, use a string attached to the dog's collar. When your dog is hungry, throw pieces of reward a few feet in front of him so he can keep his attention on them, and let him run up to a few and eat them. When he knows they are rewards and he is almost part way to one, say *hup,* and if he does not, pull on the cord. In this way he learns you have control of him. Continue until he obeys perfectly. Each time say *take it* when you want him to hop up and get his reward.

Fetch we have also considered, but in field training we must get the dog used to retrieving feathered objects without leaving a mark. Most Cockers do this naturally, but if yours does not, then remove the skin and feathers from a dead pigeon and make a model body with cut-off darning needles, the blunt ends of which are made fairly sharp, sticking through the straw or excelsior body at right angles with each other. Sew the feathers on the model and set the needles in such a way that the dog cannot squeeze it without biting on one. This will effectively train him to retrieve gently. It is amazing to see a small Cocker coming out of the brush with a large cock pheasant held high yet without leaving a toothmark on the bird.

There is much satisfaction in having a dog deliver the retrieved object into one's hand. Some dogs, in their enthusiasm, come rushing at one and jump up to surrender the object, while others simply drop it at one's feet. The proper presentation is for your dog to sit, while still holding the object, and at that point you bend over and take it.

To train him to do this, he must first have been taught to *hup*. When the dog is almost to you, simply say *hup* and reach over, taking the object. If he will not surrender it, again train with a stuffed pigeon skin with sharp needles. He then can't bite tightly, and taking it from him is easy, especially if, in the early stages of training, you slip him a small reward.

Direction is most important in fetching. I have already explained how quickly a Cocker learns the direction you want him to go by watching your arm. If he has seen you toss a dummy bird and has run to retrieve it, he will run in the direction of an arm swing, even if he has failed to see anything leave your hand.

Soon you can start using the live pigeons which you plant. A whistle will bring the dog's attention, and your pointing, which to him is the equivalent of a swing, will send him in the direction of the bird.

Most of the field work is done with whistle commands, but it need not be in private hunting. Should you use whistle commands, synchronize them with your arm motions, so the dog soon becomes conditioned to:

1. A short toot and he looks at you.
2. A long blast; he stops and sits—hups.
3. Three shorts; "you ran over—you're getting warm."

I trained a Cocker, as I do my Coonhounds, to understand *this way* and *that way*. The former meant to go right; the latter, go left. If we came to a dead end, I said this way, and the Cocker would turn right without looking at me, or left at the other command.

The whistle encourages a dog to quarter, and there are times when the grass or weeds are so tall or the rushes so thick that you won't be able to see your dog at all for many minutes. A whistle tells him where you are, and keeps him working.

When he is close enough to the bird almost to pounce on it, and you can see by his actions that he may do just that, command him to *hup,* and he will sit, which is equivalent to a point in a Setter. After enough repetition he will sit as automatically as a Setter points.

Many bird-dog men keep small lofts of homing pigeons for training. When a planted bird is *kicked out,* as these enthusiasts call turning the bird over with a foot, it will fly and greatly excite the dog. Here is another chance to make sure your dog is steady. If he is, he can stand seeing many birds "get away" for every one that is shot for him to retrieve.

To make a Cocker steady to shot, it is best to start shooting a .22-caliber rifle, and gradually increase the size and thus the loudness of the report until he has no fear of a .12-gauge shotgun. At first, shoot a few pigeons, and last of all pheasants —birds which not everyone's well-trained upland bird dogs can find.

If you live in quail, Hungarian, or woodcock country, they may have to be your game rather than pheasants. Away from game-bird farms, pheasants are so scarce in some large hunting areas that it hardly pays to train a Cocker to hunt them. If this is the case in your section, train your dog on other bird game.

Many ambitious Cockers will go after rabbits or even deer. Some will become interested even in songbirds. The crux of breaking off rabbits is simply knowing that a rabbit runs a small circle. Let him go by once, and then plant yourself and wait until the rabbit and dog come around again. Let Bunny go by, and then move on to his path, and just as your Cocker is almost to you rise up and yell *no*. Pick him up and give him a few switches. Two or three repetitions will cure him.

Cockers that run deer can be cured in the same way. And remember how lucky you are not to have a long-legged hound to try to catch. It is easy to jump in your car and listen for your Cocker's occasional or steady yipping so as to know where the deer has run. When the dog crosses a road, you will be right there to stop him. Now put your training cord on him and make a half circle until you come to the deer's track again. If the dog persists in running on the track, pull him in, scold him, saying *no, no, no,* and punish him again. Now you can make another half circle until you again cross the track, and try him again.

One of my Cockers would run a deer for hours until I broke him in this way, and in just one series of treatments on one deer track he was cured.

Another way of curing your Cocker of running off game is by hypodermic injections of a drug which causes emesis. I use apomorphine. Take your dog to a good rabbit cover. Jump on a brush pile, and when a rabbit runs out, let your dog see him, and give an injection of the drug which your veterinarian has prescribed. Let the dog go. As he runs the rabbit he becomes more and more ill, until he vomits a number of times. Usually three such experiences will cure him of running the trail of any critter which makes him feel so awfully sick.

The caution, of course, is, since you must not allow exceptions to occur, not to take him in bird cover until he is cured of rabbits. Should you start on rabbit curing and then hunt birds, and during the hunt he finds a rabbit track and runs it without nausea, it will take you much longer to train him.

The actual hunt, if you have never hunted birds or attended field trials, is best left to your observation. Go to some field trials and watch the little dogs work, then go home and train your dog.

Read the A.K.C. field-trial rules, which you can obtain by writing to The American Kennel Club, 221 Fourth Avenue, New York 3, New York. Reading matter on Spaniel trials will also be supplied by The American Spaniel Club, 19 Ridgefield Street, Albany, New York.

I think that what may impress you most, as it has so many others, is the remarkable way in which the effects of disuse have not been inherited in Cocker Spaniels. Is it not amazing how dogs whose ancestors have been used as pets and have perhaps seen no other birds than an occasional English sparrow have retained all the zest for hunting which their forebears half a century ago were bred for?

I am often asked whether only a Cocker puppy can be trained for hunting. No, sometimes a five-year-old house pet will make an admirable hunter, but since a dog's active life usually ends at eleven or twelve, it behooves us to train youngsters so that we may have as many years as possible with them in the field.

Perhaps you are a person who does not approve of hunting that involves shooting birds of any kind. If so, you can still attend obedience classes and trials, and give your dog some training if you do not care to train at home all by yourself. I suggest you buy a good book on obedience training, and read it before you attend a class.

I recommend some water work for all Cockers. They are born water dogs, and will retrieve sticks and other floating objects dozens of times if you will only throw them. If you are not averse to hunting, you can even make of your Cocker a duck dog almost the equal of a Springer Spaniel, though not the equal of the heavy-coated retrievers. It is truly amazing how the little rascal will sit in a duck blind and swim out after birds you have dropped, shake the icy-cold water from his coat, and sit shivering but ready for another plunge at the crack of your gun. What a versatile, rugged dog the Cocker is!

No apology is made for the fact that all of the illustrations in this chapter are more or less indistinct. As a matter of fact Cocker breeders are fortunate to have them. Each was copied from an original, faint from age, hanging in the old club rooms of the New England Cocker Club at 322 Newbury St., Boston, Mass. All of this treasure will be housed in the future in a special collection in the Sterling Library, Yale University, New Haven, Conn.

Chapter 18

GENEALOGY—AND A LAST WORD

Most people care so little for the past in general, and for genealogy in particular, that they can't even write down the names of their great-grandparents. Similarly, although every dog-breeding book starts off with the ancient history of the breed, I find that not one dog owner in a thousand cares at all about the origin of his dog: he wants a fine dog today, and leaves the interest in the past to the serious breeder. So this chapter is for the serious breeder of Cockers.

We should all feel some remorse over the attitude of those who care little about the past, for it signifies a lack of respect for ancestry, and hence less interest in the future of our own race and that of our dogs. To me there are few studies as interesting as genealogy. Even that of dogs has fascination because it is the history of a certain segment of life and, in the case of Cockers, life under the guidance of man.

Cocker history begins before recorded history, but we know from literature that there were *spaynels,* whether by that name or some other, long, long, ago. In 1386 Chaucer wrote, "For, as a spaynel, she wol on hym lepe." English literature contains quotations such as the following:

1410, Master of Game: "A goode Spaynel shulde not be rough, but his taile shulde be rough."
1450, Hawking: "Lete the spaynell flusch up the covey."
1484, Caxton: "A fayr yong man . . . whiche . . . had hym two fayre spaynels."
1557, Edgeworth: "It is natural . . . to a spaniel to be gentle & familiar."
1789, Wolcot: "Like crouching Spaniels, down black Lords must lie,
Whene'er admitted to the Royal eye."

By 1840 breeds of Spaniels were numerous, Cockers, Water Spaniels, Springers, and others being recognized. The first show at which Cockers were exhibited as a distinct breed was in England in 1883. In 1893 the English Kennel Club registered Cockers in the Stud Book.

In 1910 Robert Leighton tells how in 1873 Captain Arbuthnot Chloe and Alice who were by Mr. Phineas Bulloch's Bob out of Nellie who won at Manchester and Nottingham in 1873, being "shown in lightweight classes" and much of this heredity is to be found in Cocker pedigrees of today.

He speaks of "old fashioned Cockers" and how the names of Mr. Burdett's Black and Tan Cocker dog Faub and Mr. Mousley's black and white Cocker bitch, Venus, were found in the modern Field Spaniel. Mr. Burdette and Mr. Bullock crossed Sussex Spaniels with old fashioned Cockers for this purpose.

A Mr. Phillips, he says can trace his strain back to 1860 and Mr. James Farron was exhibiting successfully 35 years ago." This would bring such shows to 1875.

These old fashioned English hunting Spaniels, all in such a hurry, did not have their tails docked. It is difficult to tell whether they are hunting rabbits or birds.

The word *cocking* was not specifically an appellation for our kind of Spaniel. In 1813 Trewman wrote, "A gentleman is in immediate want of . . . Cocking dogs, such as have been regularly hunted for woodcock only." Several breeds of cocking dogs existed, and I am not entirely certain that the word *cocker* was a contraction of *cocking dog*. There was a perfectly good word, *cocker,* used as a verb. It meant to indulge or pamper a child (a favorite); "to treat with excessive tenderness and care." It must have been a very common word, too. At least as early as 1611 I find this: "Cocker thy child and he shall make thee afraid." In 1682 this: "Because thy foolish mother hath cockered thee with morning caudles . . ."

May it not have been that this next-to-the-smallest of the English Spaniels were, because of their very appealing nature,

"cockered" (pampered)? Why should this particular dog, among all the larger types used successfully for cocking, have been the one to be called *cocker?* In all the books I have read I find no better reason for calling them Cockers than the fact that their nature demanded pampering.

Thorburn's *Shooting Directory,* published in 1805, classifies Spaniels into three breeds, "the springing, hawking or starter, and the cocker or cocking spaniel." When falconry was in vogue, dogs flushed out the birds and the falcons caught them, or, if falcons injured the birds, the dogs were there to retrieve. The *Shooting Directory* tells us how the Cocker differs from the other breeds and is "esteemed for its compact form. The coat is more inclined to curl like the springer's and the tail is commonly truncated. The colours are liver and white, red, red and white, black and white, all liver, and sometimes black with tanned legs and muzzle."

Thorburn also tells us that "some of the strongest of the cockers were found in Sussex and called Sussex spaniels."

In several of the old books the account of Cockers carries a description of the feathering, and specifically states that it should be no more than that of the Setter. In the first standard adopted by the American Spaniel Club we find this description of the coat: "Flat or slightly waved, silky and very dense, with ample setterlike feathering."

In 1880 Spaniels in England were more like the American type of 1930 than the English type of 1930. The date 1880 marks the parting of the ways. The English have developed their dogs with long, narrow heads, as we have seen in Chapter III, while we here kept the essential characteristics of the first imports.

Before 1880 a few hunters imported Cockers to Canada and the United States. The Canadian dogs of Mr. George D. MacDougal of Toronto topped our best in 1881. In 1882 the American Spaniel Club was organized by Mr. MacDougal, James Watson, and others, in New York. Right then the breed started on its climb toward the top of dogdom.

There are people still alive who have been with Cockers all their lives and can remember their boyhood, when the talk about the breed involved the foundation stock. One of these men is O. B. Gilman, of Boston, whose life has pretty much revolved about his Cockers. I have "picked his memory," which is vividly keen, and so from him we have the following information.

There were some fair Cockers brought here, and most of them were centered about Toronto and Boston, even though the Spaniel Club was formed in New York. Besides MacDougal

of Toronto, Pitcher and Cummings of New Hampshire imported some, and Dr. Niven imported Black Bess and Bene. But the real beginning of our Cockers awaited the importation, by Mr. Pitcher, of a pregnant bitch named Chloe II, who was bred by a Mr. Bullock, and had been mated to a dog named Obo, whose owner was a Mr. Farrow. Mr. J. P. Willey, of Salmon

Falls, New Hampshire, bought one of the pups and raised him. The dog's name was Obo II.

Obo II did for the American Cocker what Tyndalle did for the English language: he fixed it, standardized it. All of Obo II's first pups were black. There must have been quite a few livers among Cockers of that day, since Mr. Willey boasted that none of his dog's progeny was liver colored.

Obo II. The great foundation dog of the Cocker breed in America.

Obo II's litters were large, due, no doubt, to so much hybrid vigor: one bitch, Critic, produced two litters by him of twelve pups each.

This great foundation sire started his show career at Manchester, New Hampshire, in September 1883, and by December he had won his championship at Lowell, Massachusetts. Winning and producing pups are two very different matters. Obo II did both. He sired the dog which went first at Lowell the year after he had won, the first three puppies at New Haven, Connecticut, the first three at Toronto, and first and second at New York.

Champion Black Pete.
1st., Open Class, and Special Newark, N.J. New Haven Conn., and Boston 1886.
1st., Champion Class New York 1886. 1st., Champion Class, and special for best
Stud Cocker, Boston, Mass. 1887. 1st., Challenge Class New York, 1887.

James Watson said of Obo II, "He is a nice, compactly built little fellow. His head is a little strong, but it is nicely carried; his coat is dense and flat, and his feet and legs first-class. He is a long way in front of any of his sex in this country so far, either as a show dog or sire." And, for a different viewpoint, here is what Mason, author of *Our Prize Dogs,* says about Obo II in his *criticism:* "Skull showing slight coarseness. Muzzle should be deeper, with a cleaner-cut appearance in every direction; it is wider than we like and the lower incisors project slightly. Ears correct in size, shape, position, quality, and carriage. Eyes good in colour, size, and expression. Neck somewhat too heavy. Chest deep, with ribs beautifully sprung. Shoulders strong and free. Back firm. Loin compact and strong. Hindquarters of exquisite formation. Forelegs showing great strength and set

CHAMPION BLACK PRINCE. A.K.C. No. 12524.

into good feet. Stern well set. Carriage gay. Coat showing slight curliness, especially on neck and hindquarters. Feather profuse. A thick-set and sturdy little dog that looks exactly what he is—the prince of stud dogs . . . his worth to the cocker interests of this country cannot be overestimated."

Some of the other great foundation dogs of that day, many of them sired by or related to Obo II, were Miss Obo II, Jersey,

Dunrobin, Doc, Red Doc, La Tosca, Beatrice W., Helen, Juno W., Lady of the Lake, Shina, Darkie, Black Duke, and Brant.

The first good dark red was Brantford Red Jacket, a dog of "Irish Setter colour." Particolors became popular.

Mr. Gilman rates Baby Ruth as the greatest Cocker in the few dog generations following Obo II. She was by Fascination, a

CHAMPION RED ROLAND.

Canadian dog. Mr. H. K. Bloodgood bought her after Mr. Laidlaw showed her in New York in 1895. Black Duke was also bred by Mr. Laidlaw, and was the greatest sire of that dog generation.

It is amazing how much we owe to our Canadian cousins for the establishment of Cocker foundation animals. They came to our shows and won over our breeders, then left wonderful sires and dams whose heredity was continued.

Black Duke's son, Premier out of Woodland Flossie, was bought by George Douglas, who sold him to O. B. Gilman after the dog had won first in the Open Class at New York. Premio (Premier x Lubra) was bred by Mr. Gilman, and, starting from

CHAMPION JERSEY. Whelped July 16, 1887.

these great dogs and acquisitions, the foundations of the Idahurst Kennels stock were established, and bred champions from 1898 to 1932.

Billy Payne, as W. T. Payne was affectionately known to his fellow Cocker breeders, began bringing out particolors. New York State kennels, such as Mepal, owned by Mr. Bloodgood, made champions from 1896 to 1927. Brookside Kennels made champions from 1902 to 1925, and Mount Vernon, owned by Edwin W. Fiske, and Belle Isle of Detroit, a kennel owned by Mrs. Warner, also came into the picture.

Baby Ruth. A bitch, who, it was generally agreed, had the best head of all of the early Cockers.

The period since 1925 we can call modern Cocker Spaniel history. A great many persons established kennels, and interest flared up for five or seven years and then was lost. Many were vicarious breeders, letting others do the work while they attended shows, admired their dogs, and got their names in the papers. Many were better traders than breeders. Not a few used their kennels to help out with income tax. But such are not the men and women who make a breed solidly popular, and many indeed have contributed to its decline because they wanted show winners regardless of disposition, and surprisingly few ever saw a Cocker work in the field. This is patent, for no one who ever saw a Cocker working could possibly entertain the thought of breeding a dog with long, bushy hair.

Black Duke, the greatest sire for some years following Obo II.

In 1922 one of the greatest Cocker breeders of all time began showing the get of a dog named Red Brucie. Herman Mellenthin was his owner. The dog was sired by Robinhurst Foreglow out of Ree's Dolly. Those who knew Red Brucie well say of him almost precisely what others a generation before said of Obo II. Red Brucie was shorter in back and longer in leg than his black predecessor, but, in other particulars, he had the same masculine, heavy, coarse head, the same strong back, solid body, well-sprung ribs, and large solid legs, with high, well-rounded feet. He had lean, well-sloped shoulders and a long neck. His ears were surprisingly like Obo II's and, like that dog, he pro-

Black Dufferin, a great little dog of early times.

duced excellent offspring. And of course a great many bitches were bred to him.

When his success as a sire became celebrated, others bred bitches to his sire, endeavoring to produce another Red Brucie, but no one succeeded. Brucie sired one whole litter of champions, but their dam was extraordinary, too. In all he sired 34, culminating with My Own Brucie, twice Best in Show at Madison Square Garden.

Even though he was bred so seldom, another Cocker, Idahurst Roderic, should be mentioned as one of the truly great sires. He was the son of Idahurst Belle II, and was sired by Idahurst Romany II. Roderic became a champion in straight shows, and won the New England Cocker Specialty $1000 Award for best in the breed, a feat later achieved by My Own

Many believe that Premier was the greatest foundation sire of all the Cocker breed.

Brucie. But Roderic produced an unprecedented number of champions, and, considering the few bitches he served, was probably the greatest particolored sire of all time. Mellenthin used him to produce My Own Roderic. In looking through the advertisements in dog magazines, one still finds (in 1955) the name Roderic appearing in names of dogs whose owners are proud of Idahurst Roderic in their Cockers' pedigrees. Roderic, like his mother Belle, lived for fifteen years. I own one of his grandsons, now sixteen years old, and one of his sons I owned lived to be fifteen—a wonderful tribute to soundness and breeding.

CHAMPION PREMIO. Whelped June 29, 1899.

My Own Brucie was bred to many bitches, and there have been hundreds of great dogs among the several hundred thousand Cockers bred in the last thirty years—dogs with everything a person could desire in a pet or hunter.

From 1934 until 1942 the greatest feat in Cockerdom was the winning of the $1000 Big Four Novice Contest held in Boston every year. This contest was made possible by the generous contribution of America's largest Cocker breeders, Mr. and Mrs. O. B. Gilman ("O.B." and "Aunt Sally" as all their friends called them). Here are the winners:

1934. Soabelo Cavaleade (Windsweep Ladysman—Rowcliffe Model) Owner: Soabelo Kennels, Livingston Manor, N.Y.

1935. Idahurst First Lady (My own New Model—Idahurst Highborn). Owner: O. B. Gilman, Idahurst Kennels, Dedham, Mass.

1936. My Own Roderic (Idahurst Roderic—My Own Grace). Owner: H. E. Mellenthin, My Own Kennels, Poughkeepsie, N.Y.

MEPAL'S ROSEMARY. Whelped August 22, 1898.

1937. Blackstone's Reflector (Torchill Trader—Blue Waters First Lady). Owner: Mrs. Leonard Buck, Far Hills, N.J.

1938. My Own Counsellor (My Own Brucie—My Own Vassar Girl). Owner: H. E. Mellenthin, Poughkeepsie, N.Y.

1939. Nonquitt Notable's Pride (Nonquitt Notable—Argyll's Enchantress). Owner: Mrs. Henry A. Ross, Chestnut Hill, Pa.

1940. Blackstone's Bright Star (My Own Brucie—Tarchill Terry). Owner: Leanard J. Buch, 74 Trinity Pl., New York, N.Y.

1941. Walida Black Knight (My Own Brucie—My Own Lady Alice). Owner: Mr. and Mrs. Waters S. Davis Jr., West Redding, Conn.

1942. Blackstone's Battery (Blackstone's Brucie—Blackstone's Bewitcher). Owner: Miss Florence L. Brister, New York, N.Y.

Fearless Neho. Note the slight change in type shown by this dog; another famous sire.

We have already the American and the English Cockers recognized as separate breeds by the American Kennel Club. You know my solution of the problem of the breed's decline—that problem which has preoccupied me throughout this book: those who want to continue being barbers as well as breeders, those who have created a new type and don't want to change, should, as I suggested in Chapter III, form a new breed, which the A.K.C. might accept if a club is organized. Call the new breed *Woolly Cockers*. Dachshunds, as we noted

Red Brucie, like Obo II, a great foundation sire.

before, consist of wire, long-haired, and smooths. There is room for a new, recognized kind of Cocker—the Woolly.

A revision in the old standard is necessary to permit long hair. The coat could even be lengthened by constant selection. I have seen several Cockers with their long hair rolled on papers, just as Maltese Terrier breeders do with the coats of their dogs.

I'm sure much longer coats could be developed. Some of the leading show dogs have belly hair which almost drags the ground now, and this, when lengthened further, would make quite a picture!

Winners at the Big Four. Herman Mellenthin and My Own Brucie are at the far right.

But we must remember that the coats of these dogs are just as woolly on top as underneath, so the ideal way to show them would be by an unretouched photograph of the dog in all his glorious woolly coat. This would be handed to the judge in the ring. He would give half the points to the quality of the dog and the other half to the tonsorial art of the barber. And why not?

I have no desire to glorify any particular dog, because in so many cases I have known great Cockers which were never shown. The great show dogs were great because they had the opportunity to be, as well as being of excellent type. And there

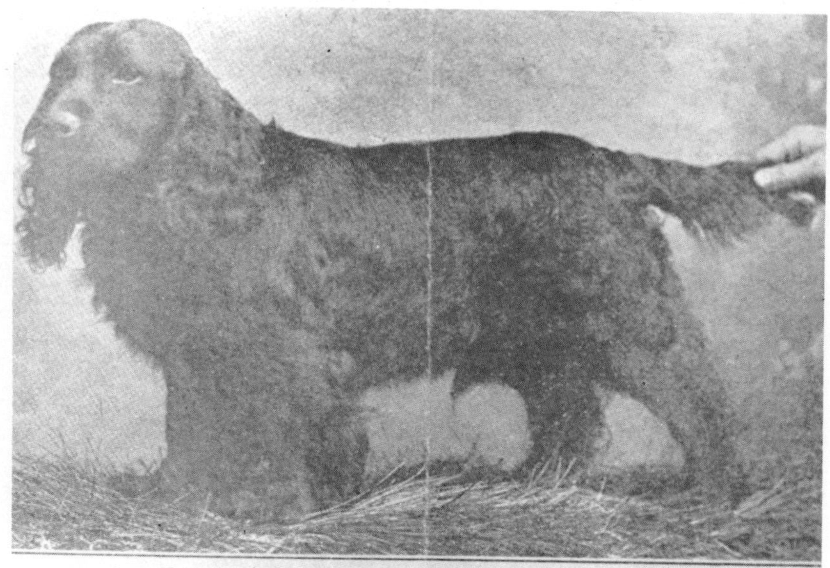

CHAMPION OBO II
Whelped August 7, 1882. A.K.C. No. 4911. Black

have been potentially great sires who never saw a show ring, were never bred, and remained as pets. They remind us of Thomas Gray's:

> Full many a gem of purest ray serene
> The dark unfathom'd caves of ocean bear:
> Full many a flower is born to blush unseen,
> And waste its sweetness on the desert air.

There are hundreds of great Cockers today which would be shown if there was a chance they could win, but their owners realize that there is no use in exhibiting against the barbered hair mops which are the victorious Cockers of today. But the breeders will soon awaken, and the real Cocker will again come into the ascendancy, and the fine type which made the breed popular will appear once more.

Here's to the natural, unclipped, non-piddling, affectionate little Cocker Spaniel. Let's all work to bring it back to the popularity it so richly deserves!

INDEX

INDEX